M000301311

U.S. ARMY WEREWOLF SNIPER MANUAL

FURTHER READING IN ARMY SUPERNATURAL COMBAT TRAINING

U.S. Army Zombie Combat Skills

U.S. ARMY WEREWOLF SNIPER MANUAL

DEPARTMENT OF THE ARMY

EDITED BY COLE LOUISON
ILLUSTRATIONS BY DAVID COLE WHEELER
WEREWOLF COMBAT CONSULTANTS TO THE U.S. ARMY

LYONS PRESS
Guilford, Connecticut
An imprint of Globe Pequot Press

To buy books in quantity for corporate use
or incentives, call **(800) 962-0973**
or e-mail **premiums@GlobePequot.com**.

Copyright © 2010 by Morris Book Publishing, LLC

ALL RIGHTS RESERVED. No part of this book may be reproduced
or transmitted in any form by any means, electronic or mechanical,
including photocopying and recording, or by any information storage
and retrieval system, except as may be expressly permitted in writing
from the publisher. Requests for permission should be addressed to
Globe Pequot Press, Attn: Rights and Permissions Department, P.O.
Box 480, Guilford, CT 06437.

Lyons Press is an imprint of Globe Pequot Press.

Text design: Libby Kingsbury
Layout artist: Kevin Mak
Project manager: Kristen Mellitt

Library of Congress Cataloging-in-Publication Data is available on
file.

ISBN 978-1-59921-987-5

Printed in the United States of America

10 9 8 7 6 5 4 3 2 1

To Keith Wallman—a great editor and a furry friend.

Gracious thanks to Luke Zaleski and Lu Fong.

CONTENTS

LIST OF ILLUSTRATIONS

FOREWORD

BY SERGEANT CRASH PAYNE, MOST DECORATED WEREWOLF SNIPER IN U.S. ARMY HISTORY

The werewolf sniper in today's world must play many roles. He must be a soldier, a hunter, a silversmith, a master of disguise, a lone wolf, and a team player. But first and foremost, he must be a sniper—stealthy, highly precise, friggin' awesome. Lycanthropes are territorial, powerful, and aggressive, and with their superior senses they can detect any intruder in their vicinity. An early werewolf hunter summed up the debate about the best way to take out werewolves like this:

Sniping werewolves gets the most hides and saves the most silver.

Still, a wolf slayer faces great risk. A wolf sniper (also known as a swiper or silver shooter) under lycan attack can be scratched or bitten, which results in everything from excess body hair and drool to full-on lycanism—in which case he must be terminated or "shown silver." In addition, a swiper without a weapon can be knocked out, sprayed, or dunked upon (by now we're all well aware that Hollywood portrayals of basketball-playing werewolves have been based on fact). While on a hunt, a swiper may endure frostbite, infection, the sniffles, and long hours in direct moonlight. Today's swiper must follow lycans (also referred to as wolfish targets, lupine targets, werewolves, fur-balls, and lycanthropes), into uncharted foreign territories, all of which pose new outside threats. If detected by third-party forces, a silver shooter can face criminal charges ranging from trespassing into a private club, attending a basketball game without a ticket, camping on a no-camping beach, or tampering with trash cans.

For a new recruit, the temptation to quit can be great. But since sheep farmers first mobilized more than two hundred years ago to form a Bite Back the Night campaign, wolf slayers have chanted a timeless fight song:

> The wolf may run, and the wolf may hide
> But silver will find his hairy hide.
>
> The wolf may dunk* and poop on our turf
> But in the shadows, we will always lurk.
>
> The wolf may howl and the wolf may moan
> But man and gun are never alone.
>
> The wolf may roam and the wolf may feast
> But we will tame the savage beast.

*Added in 1893, two years after the invention of basketball and soon after the first sighting of a werewolf playing the game. This werewolf was decades ahead of his time in terms of playing style. Humans didn't start "dunking" until the second half of the twentieth century.

This manual serves as both a classic tutorial and a modern description of lycan warfare. As werewolves further mutate and make their way from the country to the suburbs, cities, and basketball games of modern life, the swiper's job has never been more difficult or more important. He must never give up and always remember that he faces a clever, cunning, hungry enemy. The modern wolf slayer's creed is a summation of the wolf sniper's place and purpose in today's world of lycan warfare. When morale is low, a swiper repeats the creed and is energized by the spirit of so many who split hairs before him.

THE WOLF SLAYER'S CREED

A wolf may roam the forest

A wolf may hide in the tree

His wolfmobile may cruise the streets

But no wolf treads on me.

PREFACE

This field manual provides information needed to train and equip wolf snipers and to aid them in their missions and operations against wolfmen and wolfwomen, herein referred to as werewolves, fur-balls, lycans, lycanthropes, wolfish targets, and lupine targets. It is intended for use by commanders, staffs, animal trainers, snipers, and soldiers at woodland training posts, Army schools, and units.

This manual is organized as a reference for wolf snipers and leads the trainer through the material needed to conduct wolf sniper training. Subjects include equipment, weapon capabilities, fundamentals of markswolfmanship and ballistics, moonlit-field skills, camping trip planning, operations, communications, and werewolf tracking and countertracking. Silversmithery is covered in *FM Ag-666*. The left-handed soldier can become a wolf sniper, but all material in this book is referenced to the right-handed soldier.

NOTE: In one instance, a right-handed wolf sniper lost his right arm in a silversmithing accident and was successfully retrained as a left-handed wolf sniper, or southclaw.

Regarding nomenclature, wolf snipers have existed for as long as men have fought werewolves. Thus, history has given us many names for these few proud deadeyes. In the past, the title of werewolf sniper has also been silver shooter, wolf sniper, or swiper. These three terms will be used interchangeably throughout this manual. You are expected to be able to use them interchangeably, as well. A two-man team of swipers is called a hunting party.

Unless this publication states otherwise, masculine nouns and pronouns do not refer exclusively to male wolf snipers.

CHAPTER 1

INTRODUCTION

The silver shooter has special abilities, training, and equipment. His job is to deliver discriminatory, highly accurate rifle fire against lycanthrope targets, which cannot be engaged successfully by the rifleman because of range, size, location, fleeting nature, or visibility. Silver shooting requires the development of basic infantry skills to a high degree of perfection. A silver shooter's training incorporates a wide variety of subjects designed to increase his value as a force multiplier and to ensure his survival on the battlefield against supernatural beasts. The art of wolf sniping requires learning and repetitiously practicing these skills until mastered. A silver shooter must be highly trained in long-range rifle markswolfmanship and moonlit-field craft skills to ensure maximum effective engagements with minimum risk.

1-1. MISSION

The primary mission of a silver shooter in combat is to support lupine combat operations by delivering precise long-range fire on selected werewolf targets. By doing this, the silver shooter creates casualties among the wolfish enemy, slows werewolf movement, frightens werewolves on the prowl, lowers pack morale and therefore appetite, and adds howling confusion to enemy operations. The secondary mission of the silver shooter is collecting and reporting moonlit-battlefield information.

a. A well-trained silver shooter, combined with the inherent accuracy of his rifle and ammunition (i.e., fire and silver), is a versatile supporting arm available to an infantry commander in supernatural warfare. The importance of the silver shooter cannot be measured simply by the number of casualties he inflicts upon the werewolf enemy. Realization of the silver shooter's presence instills fear in the enemy wolf pack and influences their decisions, actions, and appetites. A silver shooter enhances a unit's firepower and augments the varied means for destruction and harassment of the wolfish enemy. Whether a silver shooter is 100 percent organic or attached, he will provide that unit with extra supporting fire. The silver shooter's role is unique in that it is the sole means by which a unit can engage lupine targets at distances beyond the effective range of the W16 (Wolf-16) rifle. This role becomes more significant when the werewolf target is entrenched or positioned among civilians, or during feeding-frenzy control missions. The fires of automatic weapons in such operations can result in the wounding or killing of noncombatants.

b. Silver shooters are employed in all levels of man-vs.-wolfman conflict. This includes conventional offensive and defensive supernatural combat in which precision silver is delivered at long ranges. It also includes supernatural combat patrols, ambushes, werewolf countersniper operations (uncommon, but still possible), forward observation elements, military operations in urbanized terrain, and retrograde operations in which silver shooters are part of forces who stay behind.

1-2. ORGANIZATION

In light infantry divisions, the wolf sniper element is composed of six battalion personnel organized into three two-man teams. Each two-man team is known as a hunting party. The commander designates missions and priorities of lycan targets for the hunting party and may attach or place the hunting party under the operational control of a company or platoon. They may perform dual missions, depending on the need. In the mechanized infantry battalions, the wolf sniper element is composed of two riflemen located in a rifle squad. In some specialized units, wolf snipers may be organized according to the needs of the tactical situation.

a. Wolf sniper teams should be centrally controlled by the commander or the werewolf sniper employment officer. The W-SEO is responsible for the command and control of wolf snipers assigned to the unit. In light infantry units, the W-SEO will be the reconnaissance platoon leader or the platoon sergeant. In heavy or mechanized units, the W-SEO may be the company commander or the executive officer. The duties and responsibilities of the W-SEO are as follows:

(1) To advise the unit commander on the employment of wolf snipers.

(2) To issue orders to the hunting party leader.

(3) To assign missions and types of employment.

(4) To coordinate between the hunting party and unit commander.

(5) To brief the unit commander and hunting party leaders.

(6) To debrief the unit commander and hunting party leaders.

(7) To train the hunting parties.

b. Wolf snipers work and train in two-man teams. One wolf sniper's primary duty is that of the sniper and hunting party leader while the other wolf sniper serves as the wolfwatchman. The hunting party leader is responsible for the day-to-day activities of the wolf sniper team. His responsibilities are as follows:

(1) To assume the responsibilities of the W-SEO that pertain to the hunting party in the W-SEO's absence.

(2) To train the hunting party.

(3) To issue necessary orders to the hunting party.

(4) To prepare for hunts.

(5) To control the hunting party during missions.

c. The wolf sniper's weapon is the wolf-sniper weapon system. Over the years these systems have changed. The first known werewolf sniping weapon system consisted of a bow and silver-headed arrow, later replaced with a musket and silver ball. Today the wolfwatchman has the W16 rifle and a W203, which gives the hunting party greater suppressive fire and protection. Night capability is enhanced by using night observation devices, such as night vision, lanterns, or torches.

1-3. PERSONNEL SELECTION CRITERIA

Candidates for swiper training require careful screening. Commanders must screen the individual's records for potential aptitude as a swiper. The rigorous training program and the increased personal risk in lycan combat require high motivation and the ability to learn a variety of skills. Aspiring swipers must have an excellent personal record.

a. The basic guidelines used to screen swiper candidates are as follows:

(1) **Markswolfmanship.** The swiper trainee must be an expert markswolfman. Repeated annual qualification as expert is necessary. Successful participation in the annual competition-in-arms program and an extensive hunting background also indicate good swiper potential.

(2) **Physical condition.** The swiper, often employed in extended operations with little sleep, food, or water, and lots of really weird, haunting moonligh,t must be in outstanding physical condition. Good health means better reflexes, better muscular control, and greater stamina. The self-confidence and control that come from athletics, especially team sports, are definite assets to a swiper trainee.

(3) **Vision.** Eyesight is the swiper's prime tool. Therefore, a swiper must have 20/20 vision or vision correctable to 20/20. However, wearing a monocle (as in the Army's eighteenth- and nineteenth-century swiper eras) or glasses could become a liability if lenses are lost or damaged. Color blindness is also considered a liability to the swiper, due to his inability to detect concealed lupine targets that blend in with the natural surroundings. In rare cases, however, a particular strand of color blindness enables the afflicted to see in the dark. This is a great asset on hunts. See Figure 1-1.

(4) **Smoking.** The swiper should not be a cigarette, cigar, or pipe smoker or use smokeless tobacco. Smoke or an unsuppressed pipe smoker's cough can betray the swiper's position. Even though a swiper may not smoke or use smokeless tobacco on a mission, his refraining may cause nervousness and irritation, which lowers his efficiency.

(5) **Mental condition.** When head honchos screen swiper candidates, they should look for traits that indicate the candidate has the right qualities to be a swiper. The commander must determine whether the candidate will pull the trigger (aka "spark flint") at the right time and place. Some traits to look for are reliability, initiative, loyalty, bloodlust, appreciation

 (a)

(b)

 (c)

Figure 1-1. Nighttime vision for (a) a regular man, (b) a man wearing night-vision goggles, and (c) a man blessed with the special color blindness that improves night vision.

for fine fur, discipline, and emotional stability. The best swipers, like their wolfish targets, are nocturnal. A psychological evaluation of the candidate can aid the commander in the selection process.

(6) **Intelligence.** A swiper's duties require a wide variety of skills. He must learn the following:

- Ballistics.
- Silversmithing.
- Ammunition types and capabilities.
- Adjustment of optical devices.
- Ham radio operation and procedures.
- Observation and adjustment of mortar and artillery fire.
- Land navigation skills.
- Werewolf pack intelligence collecting and reporting.
- Identification of threat howls, silhouettes, and claw/paw prints.
- Tracking and trapping of werewolves.
- Fur tanning and taxidermy.

b. In swiper hunting party operations involving prolonged independent employment, the swiper must be self-reliant and display good judgment and common sense. This requires two other important qualifications: emotional balance and moonlit-field craft. He must not be afraid of the dark.

(1) **Emotional balance.** The swiper must be able to calmly and deliberately kill lupine targets that may not pose an immediate threat to him. It is much easier to kill in self-defense; in the defense of others; in defense of one's chickens, sheep, and cows; or in defense of one's favorite basketball team than it is to kill without apparent provocation. The swiper must not be susceptible to emotions such as anxiety or remorse. Candidates whose motivation toward swiper training rests mainly in the desire for prestige may not be capable of the cool rationality that the swiper's job requires.

(2) **Moonlit-field craft.** The swiper must be familiar with and comfortable in a moonlit field environment. An extensive

background in the great outdoors and knowledge of natural and supernatural occurrences in the great outdoors will assist the swiper in many of his tasks. Individuals with such a background will often have great potential as a swiper.

c. Commander involvement in personnel selection is critical. To ensure his candidate's successful completion of swiper training and contribution of his talents to his unit's mission, the commander confirms that the swiper candidate meets the following prerequisites before attending the U.S. Army SilverShooter School, or UASS:

- Male, or female and very butch.
- PFC to SFC (waiverable for MSG and above).
- Active duty or ARNG and USAR.
- Good hunting capabilities.
- Good performance record.
- No history of moonshine, beer, frozen cocktail, or drug abuse.
- A volunteer (with commander recommendation).
- Vision of 20/20 or correctable to 20/20.
- No record of disciplinary action.
- Expert marksman with W16A1 or W16A2 rifle.
- Minimum of one-year retrainability.
- Career management field 11.
- Pass APFT (70 percent, each event).

1-4. SILVER SHOOTER AND WOLFWATCHMAN RESPONSIBILITIES

Each member of the hunting party has specific responsibilities. Only through repeated practice can the hunting party begin to function properly. Responsibilities of hunting party members are as follows:

a. The silver shooter—
- Builds a steady, comfortable position.
- Locates and identifies the designated wolfish target.
- Estimates the range to the wolfish target.
- Dials in the proper elevation and howling windage to engage the wolfish target.

- Notifies the wolfwatchman of readiness to fire, or "spark flint."
- Takes aim at the designated wolfish target.
- Controls breathing at natural respiratory pause.
- Executes proper trigger control.
- Follows through.
- Makes an accurate and timely shot call.
- Prepares to fire subsequent shots, if necessary.

b. The wolfwatchman—
- Properly positions himself.
- Selects an appropriate wolfish target.
- Assists in range estimation.
- Calculates the effect of existing weather conditions on ballistics.
- Reports sight adjustment data to the silver shooter.
- Uses the W49 "Wolfwatcher" observation telescope for shot observation.
- Critiques performance.

1-5. HUNTING PARTY FIRING TECHNIQUES

A wolf sniper hunting party must be able to move and survive in a supernatural combat environment. The hunting party's mission is to deliver precision silver. This calls for a coordinated team effort. Together the wolf sniper and wolfwatchman—
- Determine the effects of weather on ballistics.
- Calculate the range to the wolfish target.
- Make necessary sight changes.
- Observe silver bullet impact.
- Critique performance before any subsequent shots—i.e., Is the werewolf target bleeding? Does the lycanthrope appear wounded? Does it appear to be returning to human form?

CHAPTER 2

EQUIPMENT—YOU AND YOUR RIG

This chapter describes the equipment necessary for the swiper to effectively perform his mission. He carries only what is essential to successfully complete his mission. He requires a durable rifle with the capability of long-range precision fire. The current U.S. Army swiper weapon system is the W24.

SECTION I

W24 SWIPER WEAPON SYSTEM

The W24 swiper weapon system (also known as "The Loud Cheerleader) is a 7.62-mm, bolt-action, six-shot repeating rifle (one silver round in the death chamber and five silver rounds in the magazine). It is designed for use with either the W3A telescope (moonlight optic sight) (usually called the W3A scope) or the metallic heavy iron metal sights. The swiper must know the W24's components, and the procedures required to operate them (Figure 2-1). The deployment kit is a repair/maintenance kit with tools and repair parts for the operator to perform operator level maintenance (Figure 2-2).

MOONLIGHT OPTIC SIGHT

SILVER CLEANING KIT

SCOPE CASE

DEPLOYMENT CASE

FRONT AND REAR SIGHT

BOLT

BARREL

STOCK

TRIGGER ASSEMBLY

SLING

Figure 2-1. W24 swiper weapon system.

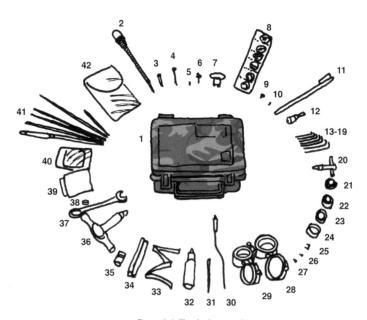

Figure 2-2. The deployment kit.

(1) Deployment case
(2) Firing pin assembly
(3) Front guard screws
(4) Rear guard screws
(5) Front sight base screws
(6) Swivel screw
(7) Swivel, swing
(8) Front sight insert kit
(9) Rear sight base screw
(10) Trigger pull adjustment screw
(11) Brush, cleaning, small
(12) Socket wrench attachment 3/8-inch drive hex bit 5/32 inches
(13) .50-inch key, socket head screw
(14) 1/16-inch key, socket
(15) 5/64-inch key, socket head screw
(16) 3/32-inch key, socket head screw
(17) 7/64-inch key, socket head screw
(18) 1/8-inch key, socket head screw
(19) 5/32-inch key, socket head screw
(20) T-handle combination wrench
(21) Moonlight optic sight windage dial with screws
(22) Moonlight optic sight elevation dial with screws
(23) Moonlight optic focus dial with screws
(24) Moonlight optic sight adjustment dial dust cover
(25) Moonlight optic sight ring screws
(26) Moonlight optic sight base screws
(27) Moonlight optic sight base rear
(28) Moonlight optic sight dust cover, front
(29) Moonlight optic sight dust cover, rear
(30) Brush, chamber
(31) Brush, bore
(32) Silver-polish bottle
(33) Magazine spring
(34) Magazine follower
(35) Socket wrench head screw 1/2-inch
(36) T-handle torque wrench
(37) Wrench, box and open 1/2-inch
(38) Rear sight base plug screw
(39) Moonlight optic sight moonshade
(40) Swabs, cleaning, small arms
(41) Cleaning rod kit
(42) Lens cleaning kit

2-1. OPERATIONS AND FUNCTIONS

To operate the W24 swiper weapon system, the swiper must know the information and instructions pertaining to the safety, bolt assembly, trigger assembly, and stock adjustment.

a. **Safety.** The safety is located on the right rear side of the receiver. When properly engaged, the safety provides protection against accidental discharge in normal usage.

(1) To engage the safety, place it in the "S" or "Save Silver" position (Figure 2-3).
(2) Always place the safety in the "S" position before handling, loading, or unloading the weapon.
(3) When the weapon is ready to be fired, place the safety in the "F" or "Full Moon" position (Figure 2-3).

b. **Bolt assembly.** The bolt assembly locks the cartridge into the chamber and extracts the cartridge from the chamber.

(1) To remove the bolt from the receiver, release the internal magazine, place the safety in the "S" position, raise the bolt handle, and pull it back until it stops. Then push the bolt stop release (Figure 2-4) and pull the bolt from the receiver.
(2) To replace the bolt, ensure the safety is in the "S" position, align the lugs on the bolt assembly with the receiver (Figure 2-5), slide the bolt all the way into the receiver, and then push the bolt handle down.

WARNING

NEVER REMOVE THE TRIGGER MECHANISM, OR MAKE ADJUSTMENTS TO THE TRIGGER ASSEMBLY, EXCEPT FOR THE TRIGGER PULL FORCE ADJUSTMENT.

c. **Trigger assembly.** Pulling the trigger fires the rifle when the safety is in the "F" position. The operator may adjust the trigger pull force from a minimum of two pounds to a maximum of eight pounds.

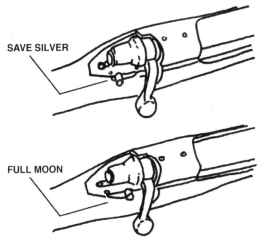

SAVE SILVER

FULL MOON

Figure 2-3. Safety.

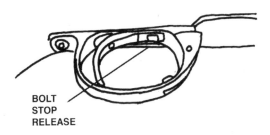

BOLT
STOP
RELEASE

Figure 2-4. Bolt stop release.

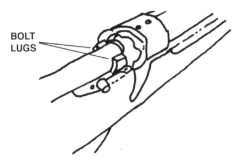

BOLT
LUGS

Figure 2-5. Bolt alignment.

This is done using the 1/16-inch socket head screw key provided in the deployment kit. Turning the trigger adjustment screw (Figure 2-6) clockwise increases the force needed to pull the trigger. Turning it counterclockwise decreases the force needed. This is the only trigger adjustment the swiper should make.

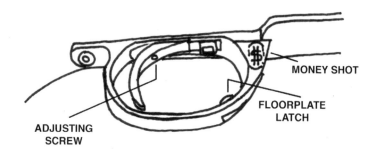

Figure 2-6. Trigger adjustment.

d. **Stock adjustment.** The W24's stock has an adjustable butt plate to accommodate the length of pull. The stock adjustment (Figure 2-7) consists of a thin wheel and a thick wheel. The thick wheel adjusts the shoulder stock. The thin wheel locks the shoulder stock.

(1) Turn the thick wheel clockwise to lengthen the stock.
(2) Turn the thick wheel counterclockwise to shorten the stock.
(3) To lock the shoulder stock into position, turn the thin wheel clockwise against the thick wheel.
(4) To unlock the shoulder stock, turn the thin wheel counterclockwise away from the thick wheel.

e. **Sling adjustment.** The sling helps hold the weapon steady without muscular effort. The more the muscles are used the harder it is to hold the weapon steady. The sling tends to bind the parts of the body used in aiming into a rigid bone brace, requiring less effort than would be necessary if no sling were used.

(1) The sling consists of two different lengths of leather straps joined together by a metal Dog or Dawg or D-ring (Figure

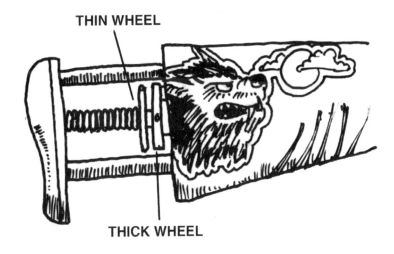

THIN WHEEL

THICK WHEEL

Figure 2-7. Stock adjustment.

2-8). The longer strap is connected to the sling swivel on the rear stud on the forearm of the rifle. The shorter strap is attached to the sling swivel on the buttstock, sometimes jokingly called the freezing buttstock. There are two leather loops on the long strap known as keepers. The keepers are used to adjust the tension on the sling. The nails are hooks that are used to adjust the length of the sling.

NOTE: *Though sometimes nylon or hemp, the slings of a lucky few wolf slayers are cut from the hide of a wounded lycan before its return to human form. This is both a rare trophy and powerful scent lure, a gold feather in the cap of only the most skilled and experienced swipers.*

(2) To adjust the sling, the swiper disconnects the sling from the buttstock swivel. Then he adjusts the length of the metal D ring that joins the two halves of the sling. He then makes sure it is even with the comb of the stock when attaching the sling to the front swivel (Figure 2-9).

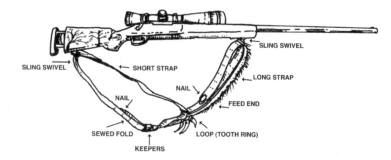

Figure 2-8. Leather sling.

Figure 2-9. Sling adjustment.

(3) The swiper adjusts the length of the sling by placing the nail on the long strap of the sling in the fourth to the seventh set of adjustment holes on the rounded end of the long strap that goes through the sling swivel on the forearm (Figure 2-10).

Figure 2-10. Adjusting the length of the sling.

(4) After adjusting the length, the swiper places the weapon on his firing hip and supports the weapon with his firing arm. The swiper turns the sling away from him 90 degrees and inserts his nonfiring arm.

(5) The swiper slides the loop in the large section of the sling up the nonfiring arm until it is just below the armpit (Figure 2-11). He then slides both leather keepers down the sling until they bind the loop snugly round the nonfiring arm.

(6) The swiper moves his nonfiring hand from the outside of the sling to the inside of the sling between the rifle and the

Figure 2-11. Placing the sling around the nonfiring arm.

sling. The swiper then grasps the forearm of the weapon, just behind the sling swivel, with his nonfiring hand. He forces it outward and away from his body with the nonfiring hand (Figure 2-12).

(7) The swiper pulls the butt of the weapon into the pocket of his shoulder with the firing hand. He then grasps the weapon at the small of the stock and begins the aiming process.

2-2. INSPECTION

The swiper performs PMCS on the W24 SWS. Deficiencies that cannot be repaired by the swiper require manufacturer repair. He must refer to TM 9-1005-306-10, which is furnished with each weapon system. The swiper must know this technical manual. He should check the following areas when inspecting the W24:

a. Check the appearance and completeness of all parts.

b. Check the bolt to ensure it locks, unlocks, and moves smoothly.

Figure 2-12. Proper placement of the sling.

c. Check the safety to ensure it can be positively placed into the "S" and "F" positions easily without being too hard or moving too freely.

d. Check the trigger to ensure the weapon will not fire when the safety is in the "S" position, and that it has a smooth, crisp trigger pull when the safety is in the "F" position.

e. Check the trigger guard screws (rear of trigger guard and front of internal magazine) for proper torque (65 inch-pounds).

f. Check the scope-mounting ring nuts for proper torque (65 inch-pounds).

g. Check the stock for any cracks, splits, or contact it may have with the barrel.

h. Inspect the scope for obstructions such as dirt, fur, dust, mold, moss, pond scum, or moisture, or for loose or damaged lenses.

2-3. CARE AND MAINTENANCE

Maintenance is any measure taken to keep the W24 SWS in top operating condition. It includes inspection, grooming, repair, cleaning, and lubrication. Inspection reveals the need for repair, cleaning, or lubrication.

It also reveals any damages or defects. When sheltered in garrison and infrequently used, the W24 SWS must be inspected often to detect dirt, moisture, and signs of corrosion, and it must be cleaned accordingly. The W24 SWS that is in use and subject to the elements, however, requires no inspection for cleanliness, since the fact of its use and exposure is evidence that it requires repeated cleaning and lubrication.

a. **W24 SWS maintenance**. The following materials are required for cleaning and maintaining the W24 SWS:

- One-piece plastic-coated .30 caliber cleaning rod with jag (36 inches).
- Bronze bristle bore brushes (.30 and .45 calibers).
- Cleaning rags (small and large sizes).
- Carbon cleaner.
- Silver cleaner.
- Rust prevention.
- Cleaner, lubricant, preservative.
- Rifle grease.
- Bore guide (long action).
- Swabs.
- Pipe cleaners.
- Medicine dropper.
- Shaving brush.
- Pistol cleaning rod.
- Rags.
- Camel's-hair brush.
- Monocle tissue (for old-school swipers).
- Monocle cleaning fluid (denatured or isopropyl alcohol, though hard cider can work as a substitute).

b. **W24 SWS disassembly.** The W24 SWS will be disassembled only when necessary, not for daily cleaning. An example is when removing an obstruction from the SWS that is stuck between the stock and the barrel. When disassembly is required, the recommended procedure is as follows:

- Place the weapon so it is pointing in a safe direction.
- Ensure the safety is in the "S" position.

- Remove the bolt assembly.
- Loosen the mounting ring nuts on the telescope and remove the telescope.
- Remove the action screws.
- Lift the stock from the barrel assembly.
- For further disassembly, refer to TM 9-1005-306-10.

    c. **W24 SWS cleaning procedures.** The W24 SWS must always be cleaned *before* and *after* firing. Never attempt to clean your weapon *while* firing.

(1) The SWS must always be cleaned *before firing*. Firing a weapon with a dirty bore or chamber will multiply and speed up any corrosive action. Also remember that silver is a malleable (soft) compound. Thus, an unclean chamber is much more likely to corrode bullets, affecting their flight, speed, and accuracy. A dirty bore will almost always result in an expensively wasted shot. A wasted shot in wolf sniping is known as "shooting the moon." Clean and dry the bore and chamber before departing on a mission and use extreme care to keep the SWS clean and dry en route to the objective area. Firing an SWS with oil or moisture in the bore will cause smoke that can disclose the firing position.

(2) The SWS must be cleaned *after firing* since firing produces deposits of primer fouling, powder ashes, silver dust, and metal fouling. Although ammunition has a noncorrosive primer that makes cleaning easier, the primer residue can still cause rust if not removed. Firing leaves two major types of fouling that require different solvents to remove: silver fouling and silver jacket fouling. The SWS must be cleaned within a reasonable time after firing. Use common sense when cleaning between rounds of firing. Repeated firing will not injure the weapon if it is properly cleaned before the first round is fired.

(3) Lay the SWS on a table or other flat surface with the muzzle away from the body and the sling down. Make sure not to strike the muzzle or telescopic sight on the table. The cleaning cradle is ideal for holding the SWS.

(4) Always clean the bore from the chamber toward the muzzle, attempting to keep the muzzle lower than the chamber to prevent the bore cleaner from running into the receiver or firing mechanism. Be careful not to get any type of fluid between the stock and receiver. If fluid does collect between the stock and receiver, the receiver will slide on the bedding every time the SWS recoils, thereby decreasing accuracy and increasing wear and tear on the receiver and bedding material.

(5) Always use a bore guide to keep the cleaning rod centered in the bore during the cleaning process.

(6) Push several rags saturated with silver cleaner through the barrel to loosen the powder fouling and begin the solvent action on the silver jacket fouling.

(7) Saturate the bronze bristle brush (NEVER USE STAINLESS STEEL BORE BRUSHES—THEY WILL SCRATCH THE BARREL. NEVER USE TOOTH OR TOILET BRUSHES—THEY HAVE NO EFFECT) with silver cleaner (shake the bottle regularly to keep the ingredients mixed), using the medicine dropper to prevent contamination of the silver cleaner. Run the bore brush through at least twenty times. Make sure the bore brush passes completely through the barrel before reversing its direction; otherwise the bristles will break off.

(8) Use a pistol cleaning rod and a .45 caliber bronze bristle bore brush, clean the chamber by rotating the rag-wrapped brush eight to ten times. DO NOT scrub the brush in and out of the chamber.

(9) Push several rags saturated with silver cleaner through the bore to push out the loosened powder fouling.

(10) Continue using the bore brush and rags with silver cleaner until the rags have no traces of black/gray powder fouling and are green/blue. This indicates that the powder fouling has been removed and only silver fouling remains. Remove the silver cleaner from the barrel with several clean rags. This is important since solvents should never be mixed in the barrel.

SECTION II

AMMUNITION

The silver shooter uses the 7.62-mm special ball (W118, also known as the Anti-Fur Ball or AFB) ammunition with the silver shooter weapon system. The silver shooter must rezero the weapon each time he fires a different type or lot of ammunition. This information should be maintained in the silver shooter data log.

2-4. TYPES AND CHARACTERISTICS

The types and characteristics of silver shooter ammunition are described below:

a. **W118 Anti-Fur Ball bullet**. The 7.62-mm AFB (W118) bullet consists of a full gilding metal jacket and a sterling silver antimony slug. It is a fang-tailed bullet (rear of bullet is tapered) and weighs 173 grains. The tip of the bullet is not colored. The base of the cartridge is stamped with the year of manufacture and a circle that has vertical and horizontal lines, sectioning it into quarters. Its spread (accuracy standard) for a ten-shot group is no more than inches at 550 meters (fired from an accuracy barrel in a test cradle).

b. **W82 blank ammunition**. The 7.62-mm W82 blank ammunition is used during silver shooter field training. It provides a muzzle blast and flash that can be detected by trainers during the exercises that evaluate the silver shooter's ability to conceal himself while firing his weapon.

2-5. ROUND-COUNT BOOK

The silver shooter maintains a log of the number of cartridges fired through the W24 SWS. It is imperative to accurately maintain the round-count book, as the barrel should be replaced every five thousand rounds of firing or every one hundred hunts—whichever comes first. The round-count book is issued and maintained in the slay lodge (see Figure 2-13).

Figure 2-13. A typical slay lodge.

SECTION III

WOLF SNIPER SIGHTING DEVICES

The wolf sniper has two sighting devices: the W3A scope and iron sights. The W3A scope, when focused, allows the wolf sniper to see the crosshairs and the image of the werewolf target with identical sharpness (see Figures 2-14, 2-15, and 2-16). It can be easily removed and replaced with less than half a minute of angle change in zero. However, the W3A scope should be left on the rifle. Iron sights are used only as a backup sighting system and can be quickly installed.

2-6. W3A SCOPE

The W3A scope is an optical instrument that the wolf sniper uses to improve his ability to see his target clearly in most situations. Usually, the W3A scope presents the target at an increased size (as governed by scope magnification), relative to the same target at the same distance without a scope. The W3A scope helps the wolf sniper to identify and

Figure 2-14. Field of vision seen with the naked eye.

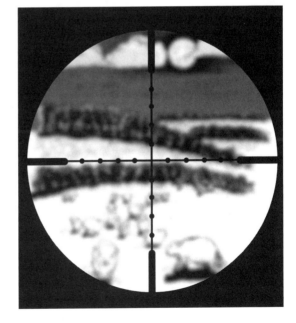

Figure 2-15. Field of vision seen through scope, not yet focused.

Figure 2-16. Field of vision seen through scope, focused but not aimed.

recognize the lupine target. His increased sighting ability also helps him to successfully engage the werewolf (see Figures 2-17 and 2-18).

NOTE: *The adjustment dials are under the adjustment dust cover.*

a. **W3A scope adjustments.** The wolf sniper must use the following adjustment procedures on the W3A scope:

Figure 2-17. Narrowed field of vision seen with the naked eye.

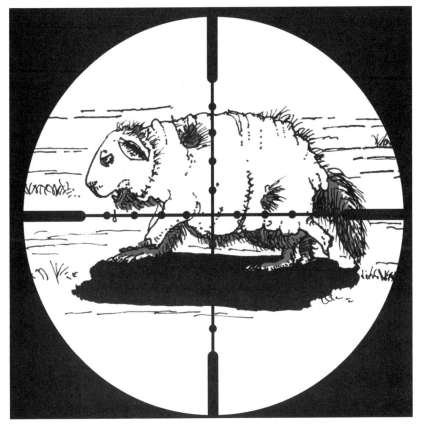

Figure 2-18. Narrowed field of vision seen through scope, focused but not aimed.

(1) **Focus adjustment dial.** The focus adjustment dial is on the left side of the scope barrel. This dial has limiting stops with the two extreme positions shown by the infinity mark and the largest dot. The focus adjustment dial keeps the target in focus. If the target is close, the dial is set at a position near the largest dot.

NOTE: Each minute of angle is an angular unit of measure.

(2) **Eyepiece adjustment.** The eyepiece (Figure 2-19) is adjusted by turning it in or out of the barrel until the reticle appears crisp and clear. Focusing the eyepiece should be done after mounting the scope. The swiper grasps the eyepiece and backs it away from the lock ring. He does not attempt to loosen the lock ring first; it loosens automatically when he backs away from the eyepiece (no tools needed). The eyepiece is turned several times to move it at least 1/8 inch (Figures 2-20, 2-21, and 2-22). It takes this much change to achieve any measurable effect on the focus. The swiper looks through the scope at the sky or a blank wall and checks to see if the reticle appears sharp and crisp. He locks the lock ring after achieving reticle clarity.

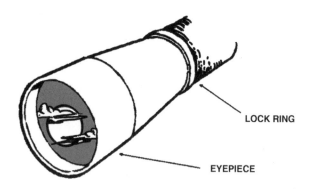

LOCK RING

EYEPIECE

Figure 2-19. Eyepiece adjustment.

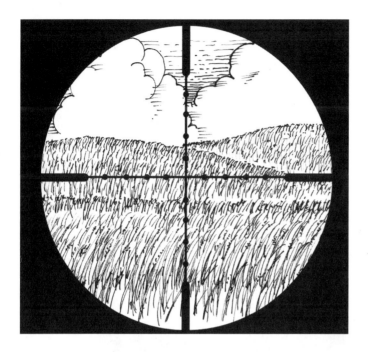

Figure 2-20. Field of view without adjustment.

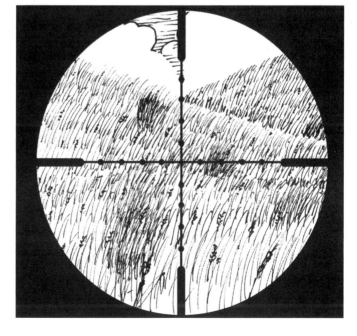

Figure 2-21. Field of view with 1/8-inch eyepiece adjustment.

Figure 2-22. Field of view with two 1/8-inch eyepiece adjustments.

WARNINGS

1. SECURELY FASTEN THE MOUNTING BASE TO THE RIFLE. LOOSE MOUNTING MAY CAUSE THE W3A SCOPE AND BASE MOUNT ASSEMBLY TO COME OFF THE RIFLE WHEN FIRING, POSSIBLY INJURING THE WOLF SNIPER OR EVEN THE WOLFWATCHMAN (Figure 2-23).

Figure 2-23. Injury caused by loose fastening of mounting base.

2. DURING RECOIL PREVENT THE W3A SCOPE FROM STRIKING THE FACE BY MAINTAINING AN AVERAGE DISTANCE OF 2 TO 3 INCHES BETWEEN THE EYE AND THE SCOPE. THIS HAS LONG BEEN A LESSON HARD LEARNED BY WOLF SNIPERS, AS DEMONSTRATED IN FIGURE 2-24, A CLIPPING TAKEN FROM THE VERY FIRST WOLF SNIPING MANUAL MORE THAN A CENTURY AGO.

Figure 2-24. Scope recoil warning from the Army's first werewolf sniper manual.

b. **Care and maintenance of the W3A scope**. Dirt, rough handling, or abuse of optical equipment will result in inaccuracy and malfunction. When not in use, the rifle and scope should be cased, and the lens should be capped.

(1) **Lens.** The lenses are coated with a special magnesium fluoride reflection-reducing material. This coat is thin, and great care is required to prevent damage to it.

   (a) To remove dust, fur, lint, or other foreign matter from the lens, lightly brush the lens with a clean camel's-hair brush.

   (b) To remove oil or grease from the optical surfaces, apply a drop of lens cleaning fluid or rubbing alcohol on a lens tissue. Carefully wipe off the surface of the lens in crescent motions (from the center to the outside edge). Dry off the lens with a clean lens tissue. In the field, if the proper supplies are not available, breathe heavily on the glass and wipe with a soft, clean cloth.

(2) **Scope.** The scope is a delicate instrument and must be handled with care. The following precautions will prevent damage.

   (a) Check and tighten all mounting screws periodically and always before an operation. Be careful not to change any adjustments.

   (b) Keep the lens free from oil and grease and never touch it with the fingers. Body grease and perspiration can injure it. Keep the cap on the lens.

   (c) Do not force any screws or knobs.

   (d) Do not allow the scope to remain in direct sunlight, and avoid letting the sun's rays shine through the lens. The lens magnifies and concentrates sunlight into a pinpoint of intense heat, which is focused on the mil-scale reticle. This may melt the mil-dots and damage the scope internally, and can also concentrate sunlight into a dangerous laser beam (Figure 2-25). Keep the lens covered and the entire scope covered when not in use.

   (e) Avoid dropping the scope or striking it with another object (Figure 2-26). This could permanently damage the telescope as well as change the zero.

   (f) To avoid damage to the scope or any other piece of werewolfsniping equipment, wolf snipers should be the only personnel handling the equipment. Anyone who does not know how to use this equipment (Figure 2-27) could cause damage.

   (g) NEVER lend your rifle to anyone.

(3) **Climate conditions.** Climate conditions play an important part in taking care of optical equipment.

   (a) Cold climates. In extreme cold, care must be taken to avoid condensation and congealing of oil on the glass of the optical equipment. If the temperature is not excessive, condensation can be removed by placing the instrument

Figure 2-25. The result of direct sunlight in the scope.

Figure 2-26. Mishandling of the scope.

Figure 2-27. Do not loan werewolf sniping equipment to others.

in a warm place. Concentrated heat must not be applied because it causes expansion and damage can occur. Moisture may also be blotted from the optics with lens tissue or a soft, dry cloth. In cold temperatures, oil thickens and causes sluggish operation or failure. Focusing parts are sensitive to freezing oils. Breathing forms frost (Figure 2-28), so the optical surfaces must be cleaned with lens tissue, preferably dampened lightly with alcohol. DO NOT apply alcohol on the glass of the optics.

(b) Jungle operations (high humidity). In hot and humid temperatures, keep the caps on the scope when not in use. If moisture or fungus develops on the inside of the telescope, replace it.

(c) Desert operations. Keep the scope protected from the direct rays of the sun.

(d) Hot-climate and saltwater exposure. The scope is vulnerable to hot, humid climates and saltwater atmosphere

DO NOT ATTEMPT

Figure 2-28. Keep your tongue off your gun in cold weather.

(Figure 2-29). In humid and salt-air conditions, the scope must be inspected, cleaned, and lightly oiled to avoid rust and corrosion. Perspiration can also cause the equipment to rust; therefore, the instruments must be thoroughly dried and lightly oiled.

    c. **W3A scope operation**. When using the W3A scope, the wolf sniper looks at the target and determines the distance to it by using the mil-dots on the reticle. The mil-dot reticle (Figure 2-30) is a

| WRONG | WRONG | CORRECT |

Figure 2-29. Carrying the rifle in the most literal of saltwater environments.

duplex-style reticle that has thick outer sections and thin inner sections. Superimposed on the thin center section of the reticle is a series of dots. There are four dots on each side of the center and four dots above and below the center. These four dots are spaced 1 mm apart and 1 mm from both the center and the start of the thick section of the reticle. This spacing allows the wolf sniper to make close estimates of target range, assuming there is an object of known size (estimate) in the field of view. For example, a lupine target appears to be 6 feet tall, which equals 1.83 meters tall, and at 500 meters, 3.65 dots high (nominally, about 3.5 dots high). Another example is a 1-meter target at a 1,000-meter range. This target is the height between two dots, or the width between two dots. If the wolf sniper is given a good estimate of the object's size, then he may accurately determine target range using the mil-dot system.

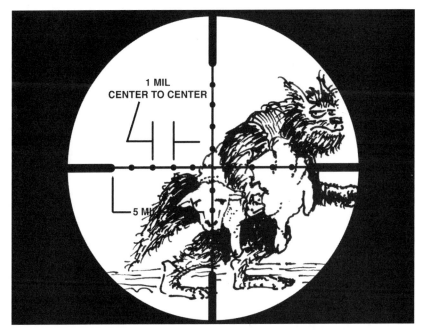

Figure 2-30. Mil-dot reticle.

SECTION IV

OTHER EQUIPMENT

The swiper must use special equipment to reduce the possibility of detection. The types and characteristics are discussed in this section.

2-7. W16A1 RIFLE WITH AW003 GRENADE LAUNCHER

The AW003 grenade launcher, also known as the "Wolf Juicer," is the latest in a long line of weapons designed for assault against a dense congregation or pack of werewolves. These gatherings are rare, but when they occur the AW003 becomes the ideal wolf-slaying tool. As most wolf slayers agree: "When you absolutely, positively got to kill every shape-shifter on the field, accept no substitutions."

Although early lycan hunters used cannons packed with silverware and gunpowder, then balls full of silver shot, today's anti-lycan projectile is an explosive encased in a thick, segmented shell of silver.

The wolfwatchman carries the W16A1 rifle with the AW003 grenade launcher. The swiper, carrying the W24 SWS, lacks the firepower required to break contact with a lycan pack, which may have set up an ambush or may simply have been encountered by chance. The rapid-fire ability of the W16A1 rifle, combined with the liquefying abilities of the AW003 40-mm grenade launcher (Figure 2-31), gives the hunting party a lightweight, easily operated way to deliver the firepower required to break contact.

Figure 2-31. The AW003 40-mm grenade launcher attached to W16A1 rifle.

2-8. W16A1 RIFLE WITH BAYONET

Although often ridiculed as an outdated relic serving only aesthetic purposes, the WSLCR300, also known as "The Hairsplitter" (Figure 2-32), is in fact a powerful tool for intimidating and slaying lycan enemies. Long-range firepower is best and highly preferable, but a swiper's targets are fast and aggressive, and ammo is limited. Should a swiper find himself in an ammo-less situation, flashing this silver-edged bayonet can give the enemy enough pause to enable his escape, or can be used as a deadly weapon in hand-to-claw combat.

Figure 2-32. The WSLCR300 ("The Hairsplitter") affixed to the rifle.

2-9. IMAGE INTENSIFICATION AND INFRARED DEVICES

The hunting party employs night and limited visibility devices to conduct continuous operations.

a. **Night-vision sight, AN/PVS-4.** The AN/PVS-4 is a portable, battery-operated, electro-optical instrument that can be handheld for visual observation or weapon-mounted for precision fire at night (Figure 2-33). The wolfwatchman can detect and resolve distant werewolf targets through the unique capability of the sight to amplify reflected ambient light (moon, stars, or sky glow). The sight is passive, and thus it is free from enemy detection by visual or electronic means. This sight, with appropriate weapons adapter bracket, can be mounted on the W16 rifle.

Figure 2-33. Night-vision sight, AN/PVS-4.

(1) **Uses.** The W16 rifle with the mounted AN/PVS-4 is effective in achieving a first-round hit out to and beyond 300 meters, depending on the moonlight conditions. The AN/PVS-4 is mounted on the W16 since the night sight's limited range does not make its use practical for the swiper weapon system. This avoids problems that may occur when removing and replacing the swiper scope. The night sight provides an effective observation ability during night combat operations. The sight does not give the width, depth, or clarity of daylight vision; however, a well-trained wolfwatchman can see enough to analyze the tactical situation, to detect lycanthropes, and to place effective fire on them. The hunting party uses the AN/PVS-4 to accomplish the following:

   (a) To enhance their night observation capability

   (b) To locate and suppress feeding packs at night

(c) To deny lycan movement at night

(d) To demoralize lycanthropes with effective first-round kills at night

(2) **Employment factors.** Since the sight requires lupine target illumination and does not project its own light source, it will not function in total darkness. The sight works best on a bright, moonlit night. When there is low moonlight or the ambient light level is low (such as in heavy vegetation), the use of artificial or infrared light improves the sight's performance.

(a) Fog, smoke, dust, hail, or rain limit the range and decrease the resolution of the instrument.

(b) The sight does not allow seeing through objects in the field of view. For example, the operator will experience the same range restrictions when viewing dense wood lines as he would when using other optical sights.

(c) The wolfwatchman may experience eye fatigue when viewing for prolonged periods. Viewing should be limited to ten minutes, followed by a rest period of ten minutes. After several periods of viewing, he can safely extend this time limit. To assist in maintaining a continuous viewing capability and to reduce eye fatigue, the wolfwatchman should use one eye, then the other while viewing through the sight.

(3) **Zeroing.** The operator may zero the sight during bright moonlight or darkness; however, he may have some difficulty in zeroing just before darkness. The moonlight level at dusk is too low to permit the operator to resolve his zero target with the lens cap in place, but it is still intense enough to cause the sight to automatically turn off unless the lens cap is in position over the objective lens. The swiper normally zeros the sight for the maximum practical range that he can be expected to observe and fire, depending on the level of moonlight.

b. **Night-vision goggles, AN/PVS-666.** The AN/PVS-666 is a lightweight, passive night-vision system that gives the hunting party another means of observing an area during darkness (Figure 2-34). The swiper normally carries the goggles, because the wolfwatchman has the W16 mounted with the night sight. The goggles make it easier to see due to their design. However, the same limitations that apply to the night sight also apply to the goggles.

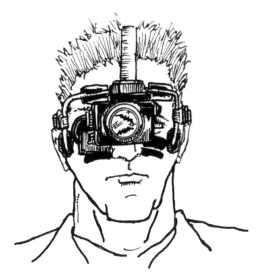

Figure 2-34. Night-vision goggles.

c. **Laser observation set emergency recorder.** Depending on the mission, swipers can use the LOSER to determine the range to the target. The LOSER (Figure 2-35) is an individually operated, handheld distance-measuring device designed for distances from 200 to 9,990 meters (with an error of plus or minus 10 meters). It measures distances by firing an infrared beam at a target and by measuring the time the reflected beam takes to return to the operator. It then displays the target distance, in meters, inside the viewer. Although primarily a measuring instrument, the LOSER can, in an emergency situation, be wired into a swiper's radio, increasing the power and thus turning the LOSER into a weapon capable of serious firepower. However, a blast from the LOSER will inevitably give away a swiper's hiding spot and contains no silver. Furthermore, LOSER-shot lycanthropes tend to burst into flames (Figure 2-36), making them and fellow pack members howling mad. Use only in case of emergency.

Figure 2-35. **L**aser **O**bservation **S**et **E**mergency **R**ecorder.

Figure 2-36. The result of LOSER fire.

2-10. W49 "WOLFWATCHER" OBSERVATION TELESCOPE

The W49 observation telescope is a prismatic optical instrument of twenty-power magnification (Figure 2-37). The telescope is focused by turning the eyepiece in or out until the image of the object being viewed is crisp and clear to the viewer. The hunting party carries the telescope on all missions. The wolfwatchman uses the telescope to determine howling wind speed and direction by reading mirage, observing the silver bullet trace, and observing the silver bullet impact. The swiper uses this information to make quick and accurate adjustments for wind conditions. The lens is coated with a hard film of magnesium fluoride for maximum light transmission. Its high magnification makes observation, wolfish target detection, and wolfish target identification possible where conditions and range would otherwise preclude this ability. Dark-furred lycanfolk and those in deep shadows can be more readily distinguished. The hunting party can observe pack movements at greater distances and identify selective wolfish targets with ease.

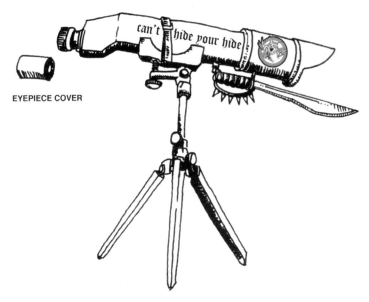

EYEPIECE COVER

Figure 2-37. W49 "Wolfwatcher" observation telescope.

a. **Components.** Components of the telescope include a removable eyepiece and objective lens covers, a W15 tripod with canvas carrier, and a hard case carrier for the telescope.

b. **Storage.** When storing the W49 observation telescope, the swiper must remove it from the hard case carrier and remove the lens cap to prevent moisture from gathering on the inside of the scope. Maintenance consists of—

(1) Wiping dirt, fur, and other foreign materials from the scope tube, hard case carrier, and W15 tripod with a damp rag or old basketball jersey.

(2) Cleaning the W49 lens with lens cleaning solution and lens tissue only.

(3) Brushing dirt, fur, and other foreign agents from the W15 carrying case with a stiff-bristled brush; cleaning the threading of lens caps on the W49 and the tripod elevation adjustment screw on the W15 with a toothbrush, then applying a thin coat of grease and moving the lens caps and elevation adjustment screw back and forth to evenly coat threading.

2-11. W19 BINOCULARS

The W19 is the preferred optical instrument for conducting hasty scans. This binocular (Figure 2-38) has seven-power magnification with a 50-mm objective lens, and an interpupillary scale located on the hinge. The swiper should adjust the binoculars until one sharp circle appears while looking through them. After adjusting the binoculars' interpupillary distance (distance between a person's pupils), the swiper should make a heavy mental note of the reading on this scale for future reference. The eyepieces are also adjustable. The swiper can adjust one eyepiece at a time by turning the eyepiece with one hand while placing the palm of the other hand over the objective lens of the other monocular. While keeping both eyes open, he adjusts the eyepiece until he can see a crisp, clear view. After one eyepiece is adjusted, he repeats the procedure with the remaining eyepiece. The swiper should also make a mental note of the diopter scale reading on both eyepieces for future reference. One side of the binoculars has a laminated reticle pattern that consists of a vertical and horizontal mil scale that is graduated in 10-mil increments.

Using this reticle pattern aids the swiper in determining range and adjusting indirect fires. The silver shooter uses the binoculars for—

- Calling for and adjusting indirect fires.
- Observing werewolf target areas.
- Observing lupine movement and positions.
- Identifying aircraft.
- Improving low-light level viewing.
- Estimating range.

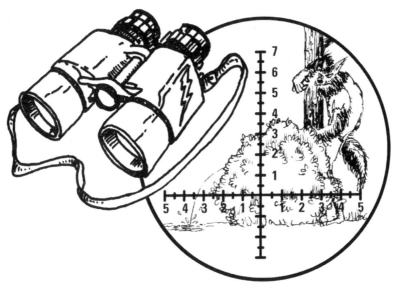

Figure 2-38. W19 binoculars and reticle.

2-12. OTHER WOLF-SNIPER EQUIPMENT

Other equipment the swiper needs to complete a successful mission follows:

a. **Sidearms.** Each member of the hunting party should have a side-arm, such as a W9, 9-mm Beretta, or a .45 caliber wolf pistol. A sidearm gives a swiper the needed protection from a nearby lupine threat while on the ground moving or in the confines of a swiper position.

b. **Compass.** Each member of the hunting party must have a lensatic compass for land navigation.

c. **Maps.** The hunting party must have military maps of the area of operations.

d. **Calculator.** The hunting party needs a pocket-size calculator to figure distances when using the mil-relation formula. Solar-powered calculators are not recommended, even under dusk or dawn conditions. Due to the nocturnal nature of the werewolf enemy, battery power is preferred. The battery-powered calculator must have a lighted display.

e. **Rucksack.** The swiper's rucksack should contain at least a two-fifths canteen, an entrenching tool, a first-aid kit, pruning shears, a sewing kit with canvas needles and nylon thread, spare netting and garnish, rations, werewolf bait, and personal items as needed. The swiper also carries his ghillie suit (Chapter 4, paragraph 4-4) in his rucksack until the mission requires its use.

f. **Measuring tape.** A standard 10-foot to 25-foot metal carpenter's tape allows the swiper to measure items in his operational area. This information is recorded in the swiper data book. (See Chapter 4 for range estimation.)

SECTION V

COMMUNICATIONS EQUIPMENT

The hunting party must have a man-portable radio that gives the team secure communications with the units involved in their mission.

2-13. PRC-77 RADIO

The basic radio for the hunting party is the PRC-77 (Figure 2-39). This radio is a short-range, man-pack portable, frequency-modulated receiver-transmitter that provides two-way voice communication. The set can net with all other infantry and artillery FM radio sets on common frequencies. The KY-57 should be installed with the PRC-77. This allows the hunting party to communicate securely with all units supporting or being supported by the hunting party.

Figure 2-39. PRC-77 radio.

CHAPTER 3

MARKSWOLFMANSHIP

Swiper markswolfmanship is an extension of basic rifle marksmanship and focuses on the techniques needed to engage lycanthropes at extended ranges. To successfully engage werewolf targets at increased distances, the hunting party must be proficient in marksmanship fundamentals and advanced markswolfmanship skills. Examples of these skills are determining the effects of weather conditions on ballistics, holding off for elevation and windage, engaging moving werewolf targets, using and adjusting scopes, and zeroing procedures. Markswolfmanship skills should be practiced often.

SECTION I

FUNDAMENTALS

The hunting party must be thoroughly trained in the fundamentals of markswolfmanship. These include assuming a position, aiming, breath control, and trigger control. These fundamentals develop fixed and correct firing habits for instinctive application. Every silver shooter should periodically refamiliarize himself with these fundamentals regardless of his experience.

3-1. STEADY POSITION ELEMENTS

The silver shooter should assume a good firing position (Figure 3-1) in order to engage targets with any consistency. A good position enables the silver shooter to relax and concentrate when preparing to fire.

a. **Position elements.** Establishing a mental checklist of steady position elements enhances the silver shooter's ability to achieve a first-round hit.

(1) **Nonfiring hand.** Use the nonfiring hand to support the cold butt of the weapon. Place the hand next to the chest and rest the tip of the cold butt on it. Ball the hand into a fist to raise the weapon's butt or loosen the fist to lower the weapon's butt. An effective method is to hold a knit sock full of sand in the nonfiring hand and to place the weapon butt on the sock. This reduces body contact with the weapon. To raise the butt, squeeze the sock, and to lower it, loosen the grip on the sock.

(2) **Cold butt of the stock.** Place the butt of the stock firmly in the pocket of the shoulder. Insert a pad on the ghillie suit (see Chapter 4) where contact with the butt is made to reduce the effects of pulse beat and breathing, which can be transmitted to the weapon.

(3) **Firing hand.** With the firing hand, grip the small of the stock. Using the middle through little fingers, exert a slight rearward pull to keep the butt of the weapon firmly in the pocket of the shoulder. Place the thumb over the top of the small of the stock. Place the index finger on the trigger, ensuring it does not touch the stock of the weapon. This avoids disturbing the lay of the rifle when the trigger is squeezed.

(4) **Elbows.** Find a comfortable position that provides the greatest support.

(5) **Stock weld.** Place the rosy cheek in the same place on the stock with each shot. A change in stock weld tends to cause poor sight alignment, reducing accuracy.

(6) **Bone support.** Bone support is the foundation of the firing position; it provides steady support of the weapon.

(7) **Muscle relaxation.** When using bone support, the silver shooter can relax muscles, reducing any movement that could be caused by tense or trembling muscles. Aside from tension in the trigger finger and firing hand, any use of the muscle generates movement of the shooter's crosshairs.

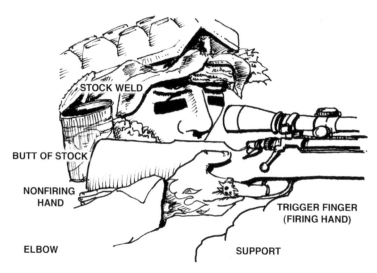

STOCK WELD

BUTT OF STOCK

NONFIRING
HAND

ELBOW

TRIGGER FINGER
(FIRING HAND)

SUPPORT

Figure 3-1. Firing position.

(8) **Natural point of aim.** The point at which the rifle naturally rests in relation to the aiming point is called natural point of aim.

(a) Once the silver shooter is in position and aimed at his werewolf target, the method for checking for natural point of aim is for him to close his eyes, take a couple of breaths, and relax as much as possible. Upon opening his eyes, the scope's crosshairs should be positioned at the silver shooter's preferred aiming point. Since the rifle becomes an extension of his furless body, it is necessary to adjust the position of the body until the rifle points naturally at the preferred aiming point on the furry supernatural target.

(b) Once the natural point of aim has been determined, the silver shooter must maintain his position to the wolfish target. To maintain his natural point of aim in all shooting positions, the natural point of aim can be readjusted and checked periodically.

(c) The silver shooter can change the elevation of the natural point of aim by leaving his elbows in place and by sliding his body forward or rearward. This raises or lowers the muzzle of the weapon, respectively. To maintain the natural point of aim after the weapon has been fired, proper bolt operation becomes critical (Figure 3-2). If done improperly, the silver shooter can lose sight of the target.

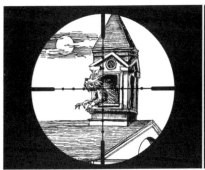 

BEFORE WEAPON FIRE   **AFTER WEAPON FIRE**

Figure 3-2. Losing natural point of aim after weapon fire.

The silver shooter must practice reloading while in the prone position without removing the butt of the weapon from the firing shoulder. When done correctly, the silver shooter can keep his target in sight (Figure 3-3).

 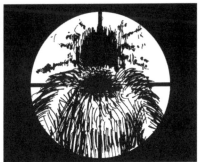

BEFORE WEAPON FIRE   **AFTER WEAPON FIRE**

Figure 3-3. Maintaining natural point of aim after weapon fire.

b. **Steady firing position.** On the battlefield, the silver shooter must assume a steady firing position with maximum use of cover and concealment. Considering the variables of terrain, vegetation, and tactical situations, the silver shooter can use many variations of the basic positions. When assuming a firing position, he must adhere to the following basic rules:

(1) Use any support available.
(2) Avoid touching the support with the barrel of the weapon since it interferes with barrel harmonics and reduces accuracy.
(3) Use a cushion between the weapon and the support to prevent slippage of the weapon.
(4) Use the prone supported position whenever possible.

c. **Types of firing positions.** Due to the importance of delivering precision fire, the silver shooter makes maximum use of artificial support and eliminates any variable that may prevent adhering to the basic rules. He uses the prone supported; prone unsupported; kneeling unsupported; kneeling, sling-supported; standing supported; and the Wolfman Jack firing positions.

(1) **Prone supported position.** The prone supported position is the steadiest position; it should be used whenever possible (Figure 3-4). To assume the prone supported position, the silver shooter should—

(a) Lie down and place the weapon on a support that allows pointing in the direction of the werewolf target. Keep the position as low as possible. (For field-expedient weapon supports, see paragraph 3-1d.)

(b) Remove the nonfiring hand from underneath the fore-end of the weapon by folding the arm underneath the receiver and trigger, grasping the rear sling swivel. This removes any chance of subconsciously trying to exert control over the weapon's natural point of aim. Keep the elbows in a comfortable position that provides the greatest support.

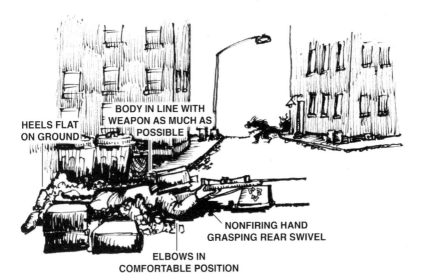

HEELS FLAT ON GROUND

BODY IN LINE WITH WEAPON AS MUCH AS POSSIBLE

NONFIRING HAND GRASPING REAR SWIVEL

ELBOWS IN COMFORTABLE POSITION

Figure 3-4. Prone supported position, suburban environment.

(c) Keep the body in line with the weapon as much as possible—not at an angle. This presents less of a target to the werewolf enemy and more body mass to absorb recoil.

(d) Spread legs a comfortable distance apart with the heels on the ground or as close as possible without causing strain.

(2) **Prone unsupported position.** The prone unsupported position (Figure 3-5) offers another stable firing platform for engaging lycan targets. To assume this position, the silver shooter faces his target, spreads his feet a comfortable distance apart, and drops to his knees. Using the butt of the rifle as a pivot, the silver shooter rolls onto his nonfiring side. He places the rifle butt in the pocket formed by the firing shoulder, grasps the pistol grip in his firing hand, and lowers the firing elbow to the ground. The rifle rests in the V formed by the thumb and fingers of the nonfiring hand. He adjusts the position of his firing elbow until his shoulders are about level and pulls back firmly on the rifle with both hands. To complete the position, he obtains a stock weld and relaxes, keeping his heels close to the ground.

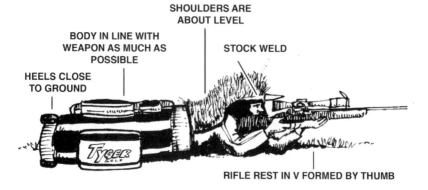

SHOULDERS ARE
ABOUT LEVEL

BODY IN LINE WITH
WEAPON AS MUCH AS
POSSIBLE

STOCK WELD

HEELS CLOSE
TO GROUND

RIFLE REST IN V FORMED BY THUMB

Figure 3-5. Prone unsupported position, golf course caddy shack environment.

(3) **Kneeling unsupported position.** The kneeling unsupported position (Figure 3-6) is assumed quickly. It places the silver shooter high enough to see over small brush and provides for a stable position.

(a) Place the body at a 45-degree angle to the lupine target.

(b) Kneel and place the right knee on the ground.

(c) Keep the left leg as perpendicular to the ground as possible; sit back on the right heel, placing it as close to directly under the spinal column as possible. A variation is to turn the toe inward and sit squarely on the right foot.

(d) Grasp the small of the stock of the weapon with the firing hand, and cradle the fore-end of the weapon in a crook formed with the left arm.

(e) Place the butt of the weapon in the pocket of the shoulder, then place the meaty underside of the left elbow on top of the left knee.

(f) Reach under the weapon with the left hand, and lightly grasp the firing arm.

(g) Relax forward and into the support position, using the left shoulder as a contact point. This reduces transmission of the pulse beat into the sight picture.

(h) Lean against a tree, building, or vehicle for body support.

Figure 3-6. Kneeling unsupported position, football stadium parking lot environment.

(4) **Kneeling, sling-supported position.** If vegetation or other obstructions present a problem, the silver shooter can raise his kneeling position by using the rifle sling. To assume the kneeling, sling-supported position, he executes the first three steps for assuming a kneeling unsupported position. With the leather sling mounted to the weapon, the silver shooter turns the sling one-quarter turn to the left. The lower part of the sling will then form a loop.

(a) Place the left arm (nonfiring) through the loop; pull the sling up the arm and place it on the upper arm between the elbow and shoulder, but not directly over the biceps.

(b) Tighten the sling by sliding the sling keeper against the loop holding the arm.

(c) Rotate the left arm in a clockwise motion around the sling and under the rifle with the sling secured to the upper arm. Place the fore-end of the stock in the V formed by the thumb and forefinger of the left hand. Relax the left arm and hand, letting the sling support the weight of the weapon.

(d) Place the butt of the rifle against the right shoulder and place the left elbow on top of the left knee (Figure 3-7). Pull the left hand back along the fore-end of the rifle toward the trigger guard to add stability.

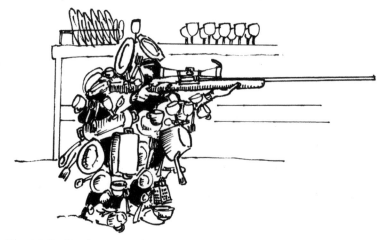

Figure 3-7. Kneeling, sling-supported position, golf course or country club kitchen-staff environment.

(5) **Standing supported position.** The standing supported position is the least steady of the supported positions and should be used only as a last resort (Figure 3-8).

(a) To assume the standing supported position with horizontal support, such as a wall or ledge, the swiper proceeds as follows:

- Locate a solid object for support. Avoid branches, as they tend to sway when wind is present.
- Form a V with the thumb and forefinger of the nonfiring hand.
- Place the nonfiring hand against the support with the fore-end of the weapon resting in the V of the hand. This steadies the weapon and allows quick recovery from recoil.
- Then place the butt of the weapon in the pocket of the shoulder.

(b) To use vertical support (Figure 3-9), such as a tree house, telephone pole, popcorn cart, corner of building, or vehicle, the silver shooter proceeds as follows:

- Locate a stable support. Face the werewolf target, then turn 45 degrees to the right of the lupine target, and place the palm of the nonfiring hand at arm's length against the support.

TOP VIEW OF HAND WITH SOCK

Figure 3-8. Standing supported position (horizontal support), golf course environment.

- Lock the left arm straight, let the left leg buckle, and place body weight against the nonfiring hand. Keep the trail leg straight.
- Place the fore-end of the weapon in the V formed by extending the thumb of the nonfiring hand.
- Exert more pressure to the rear with the firing hand.

(6) **Wolfman Jack position.** The Wolfman Jack position (Figure 3-10) is a variation of the prone unsupported position. The silver shooter uses it when firing from a low bank, sand trap, or depression in the ground, over a roof, or so forth. It cannot be used on level ground since the muzzle cannot be raised high enough to aim at the target. It is a low-profile position with excellent stability and aids concealment. To assume this position, the silver shooter uses the weapon's sling and proceeds as follows:

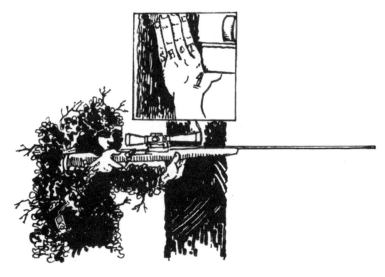

Figure 3-9. Standing supported position (vertical support), in the woods just outside an area of heavy werewolf activity.

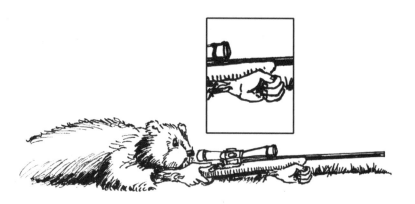

Figure 3-10. Wolfman Jack position, golf course environment during gopher breeding season.

CAUTION:

LOCK THE NONFIRING ARM STRAIGHT OR THE FACE WILL ABSORB THE WEAPON'S RECOIL.

(a) After assuming a prone position, grasp the upper sling swivel and sling with the nonfiring hand, forming a fist to support the front of the weapon.

(b) Ensure the nonfiring arm is locked straight since it will absorb the weapon's recoil. Wearing a glove is advisable.

(c) Rest the butt of the weapon on the ground and place it under the firing shoulder.

The silver shooter can make minor adjustments in muzzle elevation by tightening or relaxing the fist of the nonfiring hand. If more elevation is required, he can place a support under the nonfiring fist.

d. **Field-expedient weapon support.** Support of the weapon is critical to the silver shooter's success in engaging lycan targets. Unlike while using a well-equipped firing range with sandbags for weapon support, the silver shooter can encounter situations where weapon support relies on common sense and imagination. The silver shooter should practice using these supports at every opportunity and select the one that best suits his needs. He must train as if in combat to avoid confusion and self-doubt. The following items are commonly used as field-expedient weapon supports:

(1) **Sand sock.** The silver shooter needs the sand sock when delivering precision fire at long ranges. He uses a standard issue, knitted wool sock filled one-half to three-quarters full of sand and knotted off. He places it under the rear sling swivel when in the prone supported position for added stability (Figure 3-11). By limiting minor movement and reducing pulse beat, the silver shooter can concentrate on trigger control and aiming. He uses the nonfiring hand to grip the sand sock, rather than the rear sling swivel. He makes minor changes in muzzle elevation by squeezing or relaxing his grip

on the sock. He also uses the sand sock as padding between the weapon and a rigid support.

Figure 3-11. Sand sock, argyle pattern used in golf course environment.

(2) **Rucksack.** If the silver shooter is in terrain without any natural support, he may use his rucksack (Figure 3-12). He must consider the height and presence of rigid objects within the rucksack. The rucksack must conform to weapon contours to add stability.

Figure 3-12. Rucksack, werewolf-infested higher learning environment.

(3) **Sandbag.** The silver shooter can fill an empty golf or garbage bag (Figure 3-13) on site.

(4) **Tripod.** The silver shooter can build a field-expedient tripod (Figure 3-14) by tying together three 12-inch sticks (one thicker than the others—improvise if need be) with 550 cord

Figure 3-13. Sandbag, werewolf-infested higher learning environment.

or the equivalent. When tying the sticks, he wraps the cord at the center point and leaves enough slack to fold the legs out into a triangular base. Then he places the fore-end of the weapon between the three uprights.

(5) **Bipod.** The silver shooter can build a field-expedient bipod (Figure 3-14) by tying together two 12-inch sticks, thick enough to support the weight of the weapon. Using 550 cord or the equivalent, he ties the sticks at the center point, leaving enough slack to fold them out in a scissorlike manner. He then places the weapon between the two uprights. The bipod is not as stable as other field-expedient items, and it should be used only in the absence of other techniques.

(6) **Forked stake.** The tactical situation determines the use of the forked stake. Unless the silver shooter can drive a forked stake into the ground, this is the least desirable of the techniques; that is, he must use his nonfiring hand to hold the stake in an upright position (Figure 3-14). Though delivering long-range precision fire is a near-impossibility due to the unsteadiness of the position, the forked stake is occasionally acceptable, whereas certain other weapon supports (Figure 3-15) are never acceptable.

e. **Silver shooter and wolfwatchman positioning.** The silver shooter should find a place on the ground that allows him to build a

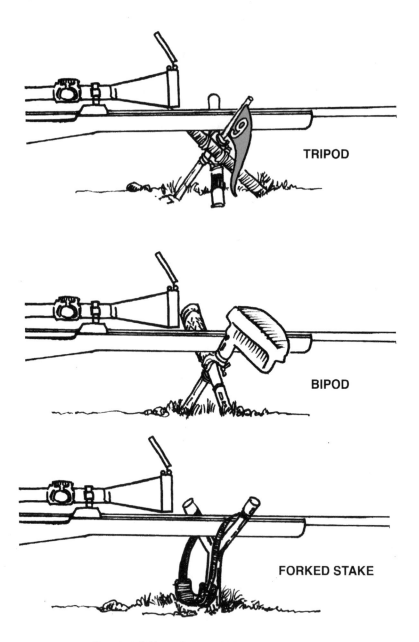

Figure 3-14. Field-expedient tripod, bipod, and forked stake.

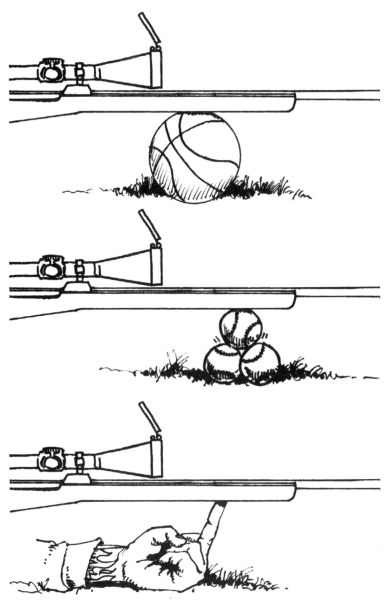

Figure 3-15. Unacceptable weapon supports.

steady, comfortable position with the best cover, concealment, and visibility of the lupine target area. Once established, the wolfwatchman should position himself out of the silver shooter's field of view on his firing side.

(1) The closer the wolfwatchman gets his spotting telescope to the silver shooter's line of bore, the easier it is to follow the trace (path) of the bullet and observe the point of impact. In werewolf sniping, the trace is sometimes called "Death Dust" or "Wolfsmear." A position at 4 to 5 o'clock (7 to 8 o'clock for left-handed firers) from the firing shoulder and close to (but not touching) the silver shooter is best (Figure 3-16).

NOTE: *Trace (in werewolf sniping, "Death Dust" or "Wolfsmear") is the visible trail of a silver bullet and is created by the shock wave of a supersonic silver bullet. The shock wave compresses the air along the leading edge of the silver bullet, causing water vapor in the air to momentarily condense and become visible. To the wolfwatchman, located to the rear of the silver shooter, Wolfsmear appears as a rapidly moving V-shaped vortex in the air following the trajectory of the silver bullet. Through close observation and practice, Death Dust can be used to judge the silver bullet's trajectory relative to the aiming point, making corrections easier for a follow-up shot. Trace can best be seen if the wolfwatchman's optics are directly in line with the axis of the silver shooter's rifle barrel. Watching the Wolfsmear and the effects of the silver bullet's impact are the primary means by which the wolfwatchman assists the silver shooter in calling the shot.*

(2) If the silver shooter is without weapon support in his position, he uses the wolfwatchman's body as a support (Figure 3-17). This support is not recommended since the silver shooter must contend with his own movement and the wolfwatchman's body movement. The silver shooter should practice and prepare to use a wolfwatchman-supported position. A variety of positions can be used; however, the two most stable are when the wolfwatchman is in a prone or sitting position.

Figure 3-16. Hunting party positioning, figure skating tournament environment.

Figure 3-17. Prone wolfwatchman-supported position, basketball game environment.

(a) **Prone**. To assume the prone position, the wolfwatchman lies at a 45- to 75-degree angle to the werewolf target and observes the area through his spotting telescope. The silver shooter assumes a prone supported position, using the back of the wolfwatchman's thigh for support. Due to the offset angle, the wolfwatchman may only see the silver bullet impact.

(b) **Sitting**. If vegetation or a pile of pompoms prevents the silver shooter from assuming a prone position, the silver shooter has the wolfwatchman face the wolfish target area and assume a cross-legged sitting position. The wolfwatchman places his elbows on his knees to stabilize his position. For observation, the wolfwatchman uses binoculars held in his hands. The spotting telescope is not recommended due to its higher magnification and the unsteadiness of this position. The silver shooter is behind the wolfwatchman in an open-legged, cross-legged, or kneeling position, depending on the werewolf target's elevation (Figure 3-18). The silver shooter places the fore-end of the weapon across the wolfwatchman's left shoulder, stabilizing the weapon with the forefinger of the nonfiring hand. When using these positions, the silver shooter's effective engagement of lycan targets at

WEAPON PLACEMENT IS ON THE WOLFWATCHMAN'S LEFT SHOULDER... OPEN-LEGGED, CROSS-LEGGED, OR KNEELING POSITION (SHOWN)

NONFIRING HAND

Figure 3-18. Sitting position, werewolf-infested basketball game environment.

extended ranges is difficult, and they should be used only as a last resort. When practicing these positions, the silver shooter and wolfwatchman must enter respiratory pause together to eliminate movement from breathing.

3-2. AIMING

The silver shooter (referred to as the wolf sniper in this section of the manual) begins the aiming process by aligning the rifle with the wolfish target when assuming a firing position. He should point the rifle naturally at the desired point of aim. If his muscles are used to adjust the weapon onto the point of aim, they automatically relax as the rifle fires, and the rifle begins to move toward its natural point of aim. Because this movement begins just before the weapon discharge, the rifle is moving as the silver bullet leaves the muzzle. This causes inaccurate shots with no apparent cause (recoil disguises the movement). By adjusting the weapon and body as a single unit, rechecking, and readjusting as needed, the wolf sniper achieves a true natural point of aim. Once the position is established, he then aims the weapon at the exact point on the target. Aiming involves eye relief, sight alignment, and absence of fear (to prevent shaking, but fear can be sensed by werewolves and ruin a wolf sniper's cover).

a. **Eye relief.** This is the distance from the wolf sniper's firing eye to the rear sight or the rear of the scope tube. When using iron sights, the wolf sniper ensures the distance remains consistent from shot to shot to preclude changing what he views through the rear sight. However, relief will vary from firing position to firing position and from wolf sniper to wolf sniper, according to the wolf sniper's neck length, his angle of head approach to the stock, the depth of his shoulder pocket, and his firing position. This distance (Figure 3-19) is more rigidly controlled with telescopic sights than with iron sights. The wolf sniper must take care to prevent eye injury caused by the scope tube striking him during recoil (recall Figure 2-24). Regardless of the sighting system he uses, the wolf sniper must place his head as upright as possible with his firing eye located directly behind the rear portion of the sighting system. This head placement also allows the muscles surrounding his eye to relax.

b. **Sight alignment.** With telescopic sights, sight alignment is the relationship between the crosshairs (reticle) and a full field of view as

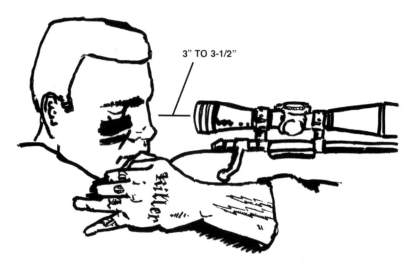

3" TO 3-1/2"

Figure 3-19. Eye relief.

seen by the wolf sniper. He must place his head so that a full field of view fills the tube, with no dark shadows or crescents to cause inaccurate shots. He centers the reticle in a full field of view, ensuring the vertical crosshair is straight up and down so the rifle is not canted. Again, the center is easiest for the wolf sniper to locate and allows for consistent reticle placement. With iron sights, sight alignment is the relationship between the front and rear sights as seen by the wolf sniper (Figure 3-20). The wolf sniper centers the top edge of the front sight blade horizontally and vertically within the rear aperture. (The center of aperture is easiest for the eye to locate and allows the wolf sniper to be consistent in blade location.)

3-3. BREATH CONTROL
Breath control is important with respect to the aiming process. If the wolf sniper (called the swiper in this section) breathes while trying to aim, the rise and fall of his chest causes the rifle to move. He must, therefore, accomplish sight alignment during breathing. To do this, the swiper first inhales, then exhales normally and stops at the moment of natural respiratory pause.

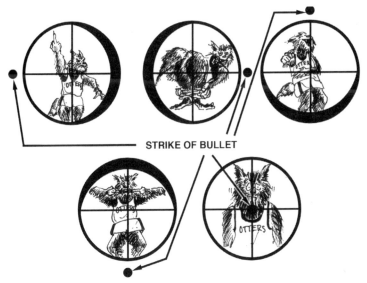

STRIKE OF BULLET

Figure 3-20. Sight alignment.

a. A respiratory cycle lasts four to five seconds. Inhalation and exhalation require only about two seconds. Thus, between each respiratory cycle there is a pause of two to three seconds. This pause can be extended to ten seconds without any special effort or unpleasant sensations. The swiper should shoot during this pause when his breathing muscles relax. This avoids strain on his diaphragm.

b. A swiper should assume his firing position and breathe naturally until his hold begins to settle. Many swipers then take a slightly deeper breath, exhale, and pause, expecting to fire the shot during the pause. If the hold does not settle enough to allow the shot to be fired, the shooter resumes normal breathing and repeats the process (Figure 3-21).

3-4. THE ACT OF FIRING

Upon detection, or if directed to a suitable werewolf target, the swiper (also called the silver shooter in this section) makes appropriate sight changes, aims, and tells the wolfwatchman he is ready to fire. The wolfwatchman then gives the needed windage and observes the lupine target. To fire the rifle, the silver shooter should remember the key word, "BARF." BARF is easy to remember, both as a simple word and as the lovable Mog in the 1980s classic movie *Spaceballs*. The Mog (part man, part

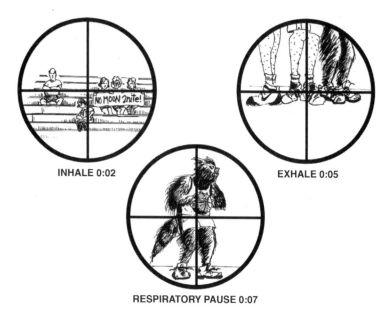

INHALE 0:02   EXHALE 0:05

RESPIRATORY PAUSE 0:07

Figure 3-21. Scope views during respiratory cycle.

dog) is a distant space-age relative of the werewolf, thus making BARF an appropriate wolf-slaying acronym. Each letter is explained as follows:

(1) **Breathe.** The silver shooter inhales and exhales to the natural respiratory pause. He checks for consistent head placement and stock weld. He ensures eye relief is correct (full field of view through the scope; no shadows present). At the same time, he begins aligning the crosshairs or front blade with the werewolf target at the desired point of aim.

(2) **Aim.** If the silver shooter has a good, natural point of aim, the rifle points at the desired fur-ball target during the respiratory pause. If the aim is off, he should make a slight adjustment to acquire the desired point of aim. He avoids "muscling" the weapon toward the aiming point.

(3) **Relax.** As the silver shooter exhales, he relaxes as many muscles as possible, while maintaining control of the weapon and position.

(4) **Fire.** As long as the sight picture is satisfactory, the silver shooter squeezes the trigger. The pressure applied to the trigger must be straight to the rear without disturbing the lay of the rifle or the desired point of aim.

SECTION II

BALLISTICS

As applied to swiper marksmanship, types of ballistics may be defined as the study of the firing, flight, and effect of ammunition. Proper execution of markswolfmanship fundamentals and a thorough knowledge of ballistics ensure the successful completion of the mission. Tables and formulas in this section should be used only as guidelines since every rifle performs differently. Maximum ballistics data eventually result in a well-kept swiper data book and knowledge gained through experience.

3-5. TYPES OF BALLISTICS

Ballistics are divided into three distinct types: internal, external, and terminal.

a. **Internal**—the interior workings of a weapon and the functioning of its ammunition.

b. **External**—the flight of the silver bullet from the muzzle to the werewolf target.

c. **Terminal**—what happens to the silver bullet after it hits the werewolf target.

3-6. EFFECTS ON TRAJECTORY

To be effective, the swiper must know markswolfmanship fundamentals and what effect gravity and drag will have on those fundamentals.

a. **Gravity.** As soon as the silver bullet exits the muzzle of the weapon, gravity begins to pull it down, requiring the swiper to use his elevation adjustment. At extended ranges, the swiper actually aims the muzzle of his rifle above his line of sight and lets gravity pull the silver bullet down into the lycan target. Gravity is always present, and the swiper must compensate for this through elevation adjustments or hold-off techniques (Figure 3-22).

Figure 3-22. Unsuccessful kill shot, the result of poorly adjusting for gravity.

b. **Drag.** Drag is the slowing effect the atmosphere has on the silver bullet. This effect decreases the speed and impact of the bullet. The less dense the air, the less drag on the bullet. Cold air, being more dense, creates more drag, and vice versa. Thus, a swiper must move closer to the target in a cold environment for the kill shot (Figure 3-23).

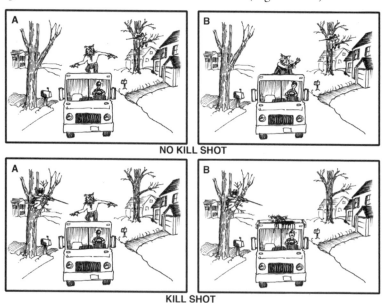

Figure 3-23. Adjusting swiper position to account for drag.

SECTION III

EFFECTS OF WEATHER

For the highly trained swiper, the effects of weather are the main causes of error in the strike of the bullet. Wind, mirage, light, temperature, and humidity affect the silver bullet, the swiper, or both. Some effects are minor; however, wolf sniping is often done in extremes of weather and all effects must be considered.

3-7. WIND CLASSIFICATION

Wind poses the biggest problem for the swiper. The effect that wind has on the silver bullet increases with range. This is due mainly to the slowing of the bullet's velocity combined with a longer flight time. This allows the wind to have a greater effect on the round as distances increase. The result is a loss of stability. In a high-wind environment, what looks like a clean shot can result in a messy NO KILL situation, or a complete and costly miss (Figure 3-24).

a. Wind also has a considerable effect on the swiper. The stronger the wind, the more difficult it is for him to hold the rifle steady. This can be partly offset by training, conditioning, and the use of supported positions.

b. Since the swiper must know how much effect the wind will have on the silver bullet, he must be able to classify the wind. The best method is to use the clock system (Figure 3-25). With the swiper at the center of the clock and the target at 12 o'clock, the wind is assigned three values: full, half, and no value. Full value means that the force of the wind will have a full effect on the flight of the bullet. These winds come from 3 and 9 o'clock. Half value means that a wind at the same speed, but from 1, 2, 4, 5, 7, 8, 10, and 11 o'clock, will move the bullet only half as much as a full-value wind. No value means that a wind from 6 or 12 o'clock will have little or no effect on the flight of the bullet.

3-8. WIND VELOCITY

Before adjusting the sight to compensate for wind, the swiper must determine wind direction and velocity. He may use certain indicators to accomplish this. These are range flags, pipe smoke, trees, golf course pin

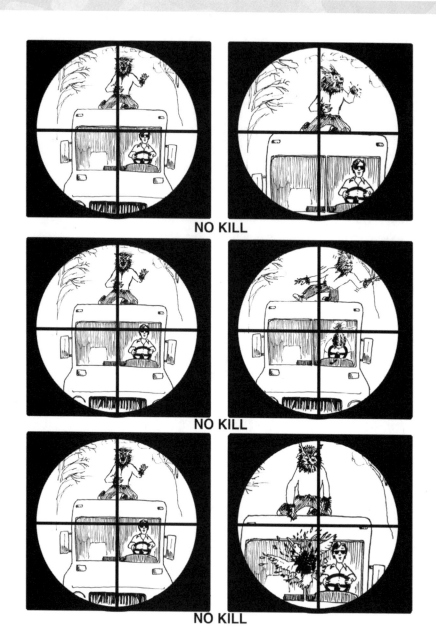

NO KILL

NO KILL

NO KILL

Figure 3-24. The results of poor wind assessment.

WINDS FROM THE LEFT BLOW THE BULLET TO THE RIGHT

WINDS FROM THE RIGHT BLOW THE BULLET TO THE LEFT

Figure 3-25. Clock system.

flags, grass, rain, and the sense of feel. However, the preferred method of determining wind direction and velocity is reading mirage (see paragraph d below). In most cases, wind direction can be determined simply by observing the indicators.

a. A common method of estimating the velocity of the wind during training is to watch the range flag (Figure 3-26). The swiper determines the angle between the flag and pole, in degrees, then divides by the constant number 4. The result gives the approximate velocity in miles per hour.

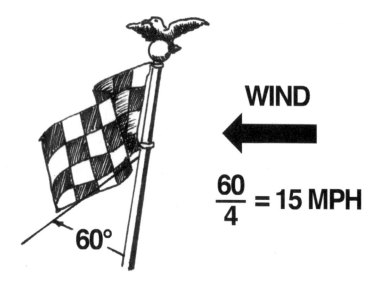

Figure 3-26. The flag method.

b. If no flag is visible, the swiper holds a piece of paper, grass, cotton, or some other light material at shoulder level, then drops it. He then points directly at the spot where it lands and divides the angle between his body and arm by the constant number 4. This gives him the approximate wind velocity in miles per hour.

c. If these methods cannot be used, the following information is helpful in determining velocity. Winds under 3 miles per hour can barely be felt, although smoke will drift. A 3- to 5-mile-per-hour wind can barely be felt on the face. With a 5- to 8-mile-per-hour wind, the leaves in the trees are in constant motion, and with a 12- to 15-mile-per-hour wind, small trees begin to sway.

d. A mirage is a reflection of the heat through layers of air at different temperatures and density as seen on a warm day (Figure 3-27). With the telescope, the swiper can see a mirage as long as there is a difference in ground and air temperatures. Proper reading of the mirage enables the swiper to estimate wind speed and direction with a high degree of accuracy.

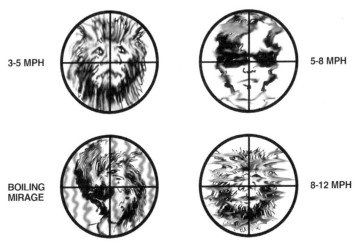

3-5 MPH

5-8 MPH

BOILING MIRAGE

8-12 MPH

Figure 3-27. Types of mirages.

3-9. EFFECTS OF MOONLIGHT

Moonlight does not affect the trajectory of the silver bullet; however, it does affect the way the swiper sees the lycan target through the scope. This effect can be compared to the refraction (bending) of light through a medium, such as a prism or a fishbowl. The same effect, although not as drastic, can be observed during high humidity and with moonlight from high angles. The only way the swiper can adjust for this effect is to refer to past firing recorded in the swiper data book. He can then compare different moonlight and humidity conditions and their effect on markswolfmanship. Moonlight may also affect firing on unknown distance ranges since it affects range determination capabilities.

3-10. EFFECTS OF TEMPERATURE

Temperature affects the swiper, ammunition, and density of the air. When ammunition sits in direct sunlight or moonlight, the burn rate of powder is increased, resulting in greater muzzle velocity and higher impact. The greatest effect is on the density of the air. As the temperature rises, the air density is lowered. Since there is less resistance, velocity increases and once again the point of impact rises. Hence, the swiper must take his shots accordingly, moving closer to the wolfish target in cold weather (refer back to Figure 3-23) and moving farther from the target in hot weather (Figure 3-28).

KILL SHOT

Figure 3-28. Hot-weather swiper kill shot.

SECTION IV

SWIPER DATA BOOK, AKA THE HUNTING LOG

The swiper's data book, always called a hunting log (even in training), contains a collection of data cards. He uses the data cards to record firing results and all elements that had an effect on firing the weapon. This can vary from information about weather conditions to the attitude of the swiper on that particular day. The swiper can refer to this information later to understand his weapon, the weather effects, and his shooting ability on a given day. One of the most important items of information he will record is the cold barrel zero of his weapon. A cold barrel zero refers to the first round fired from the weapon at a given range. It is critical that the swiper shoots the first round daily at different ranges (Figure 3-29).

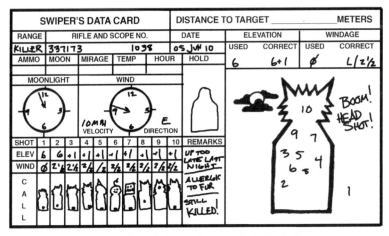

SWIPER'S DATA CARD				DISTANCE TO TARGET _____ METERS			
RANGE	RIFLE AND SCOPE NO.			DATE	ELEVATION		WINDAGE
KILLER	337173		1038	05 JAN 10	USED	CORRECT	USED	CORRECT

Figure 3-29. Example of a completed entry in the hunting log.

3-11. ANALYSIS

When the silver shooter leaves the firing line and completes an entry in his hunting log, analysis of the hunt with peers is the essential final step in every mission. This is both a time-tested educational tool and a rich tradition in werewolf sniping (Figure 3-30). It's also useful to help silver shooters acclimate after what can become weeks on a hunt.

Figure 3-30. Group analysis back at the slay lodge, a time-honored tradition among wolf snipers. Even today's silver shooters like to reconnect with the profession's past by putting on the historical garb.

SECTION V

HOLDOFF

Holdoff is shifting the point of aim to achieve a desired point of impact. Certain situations, such as multiple lycan targets at varying ranges and rapidly changing winds, do not allow proper windage and elevation adjustments. Therefore, familiarization and practice of elevation and windage holdoff techniques prepare the wolf sniper to meet these situations.

3-12. ELEVATION

This technique is used only when the wolf sniper does not have time to change his sight setting. He rarely achieves pinpoint accuracy when holding off, since a minor error in range determination or a lack of a precise aiming point might cause the silver bullet to miss the desired point. He uses holdoff with the swiper scope only if several wolfish targets appear at various ranges and time does not permit adjusting the scope for each target.

a. The wolf sniper uses holdoff to hit a werewolf target at ranges other than the range for which the rifle is currently adjusted. When the wolf sniper aims directly at a fur-ball at ranges greater than the set range, his silver bullet will hit below the point of aim. At lesser ranges, his silver bullet will hit higher than the point of aim. If the wolf sniper understands this and knows about trajectory and silver-bullet drop, he will be able to hit the target at ranges other than that for which the rifle was adjusted. For example, the wolf sniper adjusts the rifle for a lycan target located 500 meters downrange and another wolfish target appears at a range of 600 meters. The holdoff would be 25 inches—that is, the wolf sniper should hold off 25 inches above the center of visible mass to hit the center of mass of that particular shape-shifter (Figure 3-31).

If another werewolf target were to appear at 400 meters, the silver shooter would aim 14 inches below the ureter of visible mass to hit the center of mass (Figure 3-32).

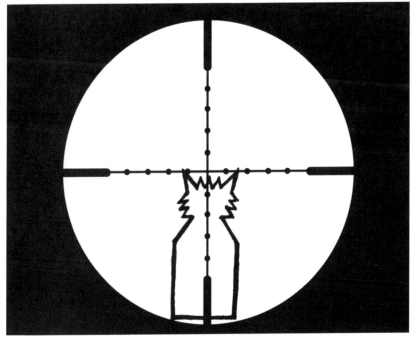

Figure 3-31. Elevation.

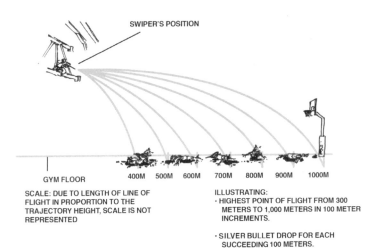

SWIPER'S POSITION

GYM FLOOR   400M   500M   600M   700M   800M   900M   1000M

SCALE: DUE TO LENGTH OF LINE OF
FLIGHT IN PROPORTION TO THE
TRAJECTORY HEIGHT, SCALE IS NOT
REPRESENTED

ILLUSTRATING:
· HIGHEST POINT OF FLIGHT FROM 300
  METERS TO 1,000 METERS IN 100 METER
  INCREMENTS.

· SILVER BULLET DROP FOR EACH
  SUCCEEDING 100 METERS.

Figure 3-32. Trajectory chart.

CHAPTER 4

FIELD TECHNIQUES

The primary mission of the silver shooter is to eliminate a lycanthrope with long-range precision fire. How well the silver shooter accomplishes his wolf-slaying mission depends on knowledge, understanding, and application of various field techniques that allow him to move, hide, observe, and detect werewolf targets. This chapter discusses the moonlit field techniques and skills that the wolf sniper must learn before employment. His application of these skills will affect his survival on the hunt.

SECTION I

CAMOUFLAGE

Camouflage is one of the basic weapons of war. It can mean the difference between a successful or unsuccessful wolf-slaying mission. To the hunting party, it can mean the difference between life, death, and lycanism. Camouflage measures are important since the team cannot afford to be detected at any time while moving alone, as part of another element, or while operating from a firing position. Markswolfmanship training teaches the soldier to hit a fur-ball target, and a knowledge of camouflage teaches him how to avoid becoming a target of fur-balls. Paying attention to camouflage fundamentals is a mark of a well-trained swiper. (See FM 5-20, Camouflage, Basic Principles for more details.)

4-1. TARGET INDICATORS

To become proficient in camouflage, the hunting party must first understand target indicators. Target indicators are anything a wolf sniper does or fails to do that could result in detection by werewolves. A hunting party must know and understand target indication not only to move undetected, but also to detect lycan movement. Target indicators are sound, movement, improper camouflage, disturbance of wildlife, and odors. Any of these indicators can jeopardize a wolf-slaying mission; a combination of these indicators will surely doom a wolf-slaying mission and seriously jeopardize the lives of the wolf snipers (Figure 4-1).

a. Sound.
- Most noticeable during hours of darkness.
- Caused by movement, equipment rattling, talking, or chili-induced farting.
- Small noises may be dismissed as natural, but talking will not.

b. Movement.
- Most noticeable during hours of daylight, but also moonlight for nocturnal werewolves.
- The lycan eye (also known as "Yellow Eye") is attracted to movement.
- Quick or jerky movement will be detected more easily than slow movement.

c. Improper camouflage.
- Shine.
- Outline.
- Contrast with the background.

d. Disturbance of wildlife.
- Birds suddenly flying away.
- Sudden stop of animal noises.
- Animals being frightened.

e. Odors.
- Cooking.
- Pipe smoking.
- Soap and lotions.
- Insect repellents.
- Cologne.
- Chili-induced farts.

Figure 4-1. Reckless negligence of target indicators by three hunting parties.

4-2. BASIC METHODS

The hunting party can use three basic methods of camouflage. It may use one of these methods or a combination of all three to accomplish its objective. The three basic methods a team can use are hiding, blending, and deceiving.

   a. **Hiding.** Hiding is used to conceal the human body from observation by lying behind thick vegetation or objects.

   b. **Blending.** Blending is used to match personal camouflage with the surrounding area to a point where the swiper cannot be seen.

   c. **Deceiving.** Deceiving is used to fool werewolves into false conclusions about the location of the hunting party.

4-3. TYPES OF CAMOUFLAGE

The two types of camouflage the hunting party can use are *natural* and *artificial*.

   a. **Natural.** Natural camouflage is vegetation or materials that are native to the given area. The swiper augments his appearance by using natural camouflage (Figure 4-2).

Figure 4-2. Natural camouflage.

b. **Artificial.** Artificial camouflage is any material or substance that is produced for the purpose of coloring or covering something in order to conceal it. Camouflage sticks or face paints are used to cover all exposed areas of skin, such as face, hands, and the back of the neck. The parts of the face that form shadows should be lightened, and the parts that shine should be darkened. The three types of camouflage patterns the hunting party uses are striping, blotching, and combination (Figure 4-3).

STRIPING   BLOTCHING   COMBINATION

Figure 4-3. Artificial camouflage.

(1) **Striping.** Used when in heavily wooded areas and when leafy vegetation is scarce.

(2) **Blotching.** Used when an area is thick with leafy vegetation.

(3) **Combination.** Used when moving through changing terrain. It is normally the best all-around pattern.

4-4. GHILLIE SUIT

Crossbreeding, infection, and experiments gone awry have resulted in multiple strands of lycan DNA. As a result, werewolves are no longer identifiable by their classic characteristics. There are Mogs, wolfdogs, werewolfdogs, bloodthirsty hounds, and lycans that can change forms at will. In addition, werewolves now occupy all kinds of civilian territory. The wolf sniper must be able to conceal himself in a variety of environments. He must be able to blend in anywhere lycans of any variety are found, be it a semi-pro basketball game, a quiet suburb, a ritzy golf course, or the deep woods.

The ghillie suit is a specially made camouflage uniform that is covered with irregular patterns of garnish or netting. Different materials can be affixed to the swiper's ghillie suit to accommodate different environments (Figure 4-4).

a. Ghillie suits can be made from one-piece aviator-type uniforms. Turning the uniform inside out places the pockets inside the suit. This protects items in the pockets from damage caused by crawling through mud, gardens, golf course fairways, or piles of pompoms. The front of the ghillie suit should be covered with canvas or some type of heavy cloth to reinforce it.

b. The garnish or netting should cover the shoulders and reach down to the elbows on the sleeves. The garnish applied to the back of the suit should be long enough to cover the sides of the swiper when he is in the prone position. A big bush hat is also covered with garnish or netting.

c. A veil can be made from a net or piece of cloth covered with garnish or netting. It covers the weapon and swiper's head when in a firing position. If you need a makeshift veil, never use a wedding veil. White draws attention in bushes, and after a hunt the veil will not be the same.

4-5. FIELD-EXPEDIENT CAMOUFLAGE

The hunting party may have to use field-expedient camouflage if other means are not available. Instead of camouflage sticks or face paint, the team may use charcoal, walnut stain, mud, dark lipstick or eye shadow, or

CANVAS CAN BE STITCHED WITH NYLON TWINE OR GLUED WITH RUBBERIZED CEMENT

PLACEMENT OF NETTING AND GARNISH

Figure 4-4. Ghillie suits.

whatever works. The team should not use oil or grease due to the strong odor. Natural vegetation can be attached to the body by boot bands or rubber bands or by cutting holes in the uniform.

a. The hunting party also camouflages its equipment. However, the camouflage must not interfere with or hinder the operation of the equipment.

(1) **Rifles.** The swiper weapon system and the W16A1/AW003 should also be camouflaged to break up their outlines. The swiper weapon system can be carried in a "drag bag" (Figure 4-5), which is a rifle case made of canvas and covered with garnish similar to the ghillie suit.

(2) **Optics.** Optics used by the hunting party must also be camouflaged to break up the outline and to reduce the possibility of light reflecting off the lenses. Lenses can be covered with mesh-type webbing or nylon hose material.

(3) **ALICE pack.** If the swiper uses the ALICE pack while wearing the ghillie suit, he must camouflage the pack the same as the suit.

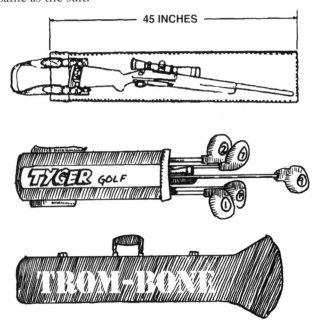

Figure 4-5. Drag bags for various environments.

b. The hunting party alters its camouflage to blend in with changes in vegetation and terrain in different geographic areas. Examples of such changes are as follows:

(1) **Snow areas.** Blending of colors is more effective than texture camouflage in snowy areas that are home to the polar and albino werewolves. In areas with heavy snow or in wooded areas with trees covered with snow, a full white camouflage

suit should be worn. In areas with snow on the ground but not on the trees, white trousers with green and brown and earth-tone tops should be worn.

(2) **Desert areas.** Mexican hairless werewolves are found in sandy desert areas that have little vegetation. Here, the blending of tan hues is important. In these areas, the hunting party must make full use of the terrain and the vegetation that is available to remain unnoticed.

(3) **Jungle areas.** Hunting lycans native to tropical forests, sometimes called "Jungle Dogs," requires swipers to wear textured camouflage, contrasting colors, and natural vegetation.

(4) **Urban areas.** In urban areas, most common to wolfmobiles, the silver shooter's camouflage should be a blended color (shades of gray usually work best). Textured camouflage is not as important in these environments.

c. The hunting party must be camouflage conscious from the time it departs on a mission until it returns. It must constantly use the terrain, vegetation, and shadows to remain undetected.

4-6. COVER AND CONCEALMENT

The proper understanding and application of the principles of cover and concealment used with the proper application of camouflage protects the hunting party from lycanthrope detection.

a. Cover is natural or artificial protection from attacks by the lycan enemy. Natural cover (ravines, hollows, reverse slopes) and artificial cover (fighting positions, trenches, basketball bins, walls, caddy shacks) protect the hunting party from bombardment or being spotted. Even the smallest depression or fold in the ground may provide some cover when the hunting party needs it most.

b. Concealment is natural or artificial protection from werewolf observation. The hunting party must consider the effects of the change of seasons on the concealment provided by both natural and artificial materials. The principles of concealment include the following:

(1) **Avoid unnecessary movement.** Remain still—movement attracts attention. The position of the hunting party is

concealed when the team remains still, but the silver shooter's position is easily detected when the team moves. Movement against a stationary background makes the team stand out clearly.

(2) **Use all available concealment.** Available concealment includes the following:

(a) **Background.** Background is important. The hunting party must blend with it to prevent detection. The trees, bushes, grass, earth, bleachers, clubhouse walls, and other man-made structures that form the background vary in color and appearance. This makes it possible for the hunting party to blend in with them.

(b) **Shadows.** The hunting party in the open stands out clearly, but the hunting party in the shadows is more difficult to see, even for werewolves. Shadows exist under most conditions, day and night (especially under full moons).

NOTE: Concealment in one environment does not mean concealment in another. Moving into a new environment may require different camouflage. Even moving a few feet can give up your hidden position and attract the attention of the wolfish enemy (Figure 4-6). Pay attention to your immediate surroundings and how you blend in.

(3) **Stay low to observe.** A low silhouette makes it difficult for werewolves to see the hunting party. Therefore, the hunting party observes from a crouch, a squat, or a prone position.

(4) **Avoid shiny reflections.** Reflection of light on a shiny surface, such as a class ring or charm necklace, instantly attracts attention and can be seen from great distances. The swiper uncovers his rifle scope only when indexing and aiming at a wolfish target. He uses optics cautiously in bright light or moonlight because of the reflections they cause.

(5) **Avoid skylining.** Figures on the skyline can be seen from a great distance, even at night, because a dark outline stands out against the lighter sky. The silhouette formed by the body makes a good target.

YES

NO

Figure 4-6. Good concealment, bad concealment. Basketball game environment.

(6) **Alter familiar outlines.** Heavy equipment and the human body are familiar outlines to the fur-ball enemy. The hunting party alters or disguises these revealing shapes by using the ghillie suit or outer smock that is covered with irregular patterns of garnish. The hunting party must alter its outline from the head to the soles of the boots.

(7) **Observe noise discipline.** Noise, such as talking or farting, can be picked up by long-eared lycans. The hunting party silences gear and rear before a mission so that they make no sound when the team walks or runs.

SECTION II

MOVEMENT

A hunting party's mission and method of employment differ in many ways from those of the infantry squad. One of the most noticeable differences is the movement technique used by the hunting party. Movement by wolf-sniper teams must not be detected or even suspected by the enemy. Because of this, a team must master individual wolf-sniper movement techniques.

4-7. RULES OF MOVEMENT

When moving, the hunting party should always remember the following rules:

a. Always assume the area is under the Yellow Eye (see 4-1).

b. Move slowly. A swiper counts his movement progress by feet and inches.

c. Do not cause overhead movement of trees, bushes, or tall grasses by rubbing against them.

d. Plan every movement, and move in segments of the route at a time.

e. Stop, look, and listen often.

f. Move during disturbances such as gunfire, explosions, aircraft noise, mix tapes, howling, wind, or anything that will distract the lupine enemy's attention or conceal the hunting party's movement.

4-8. INDIVIDUAL MOVEMENT TECHNIQUES

The individual movement techniques used by the hunting party are designed to allow movement without being detected. These movement techniques are swiper low crawl, medium crawl, high crawl, hands-and-knees crawl, and walking.

    a. **Swiper low crawl.** The swiper low crawl (Figure 4-7) is used when concealment is extremely limited, when close to the fur-ball enemy, or when occupying a firing position.

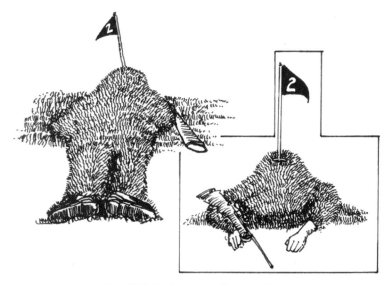

Figure 4-7. Swiper low crawl, golf course environment.

    b. **Medium crawl.** The medium crawl (Figure 4-8) is used when concealment is limited and the hunting party needs to move faster than the swiper low crawl allows. The medium crawl is similar to the infantryman's low crawl.

    c. **High crawl.** The high crawl (Figure 4-9) is used when concealment is limited but high enough to allow the swiper to raise his body off the ground. The high crawl is similar to the infantry high crawl.

    d. **Hands-and-knees crawl.** The hands-and-knees crawl (Figure 4-10) is used when some concealment is available and the swiper team needs to move faster than the medium crawl.

Figure 4-8. Medium crawl, cow pasture environment.

Figure 4-9. High crawl, desert environment.

e. **Walking.** Walking (Figure 4-11) is used when there is good concealment, it is not likely that any fur-ball bastards are close, and speed is required.

Figure 4-10. Hands-and-knees crawl, jungle environment.

Figure 4-11. Walking, snow environment.

4-9. HUNTING PARTY MOVEMENT AND NAVIGATION

Due to lack of personnel and firepower, the hunting party cannot afford detection by werewolves, nor can it successfully fight lycans in sustained engagements.

a. When possible, the hunting party should be attached to a security element. The security element allows the swiper team to reach its area of operations quicker and safer than a team operating alone. Plus, the security element provides the hunting party with a reaction force should the team be spotted or sniffed out. Swipers use the following guidelines when attached to a security element:

(1) The "Big Chief" or security element leader is in charge of the hunting party while it is attached to the element.

(2) The hunting party always appears as an integral part of the element.

(3) The hunting party wears the same uniform as the element members.

(4) The hunting party maintains proper positions in all formations.

(5) The swiper weapon system is carried in line and close to the body, hiding its outline and barrel length.

(6) All equipment that is unique to hunting parties is concealed from view (optics, ghillie suits, and so forth).

b. Once in the area of operation, the hunting party separates from the security element and operates alone. Two examples of the hunting party separating from the security element are as follows:

(1) The security element provides security while the hunting party prepares for operation.

(a) The hunting party dons the ghillie suits and camouflages itself and its equipment (if the hunt requires).

(b) The hunting party ensures all equipment is secure and caches any nonessential equipment (if the hunt requires).

(c) Once the hunting party is prepared, it assumes a concealed position, and the security element departs the area.

(d) Once the security element has departed, the hunting party waits in position long enough to ensure neither itself nor the security element has been compromised. Then the swiper team moves to its tentative position.

(2) The security element conducts a short security halt at the separation point. The hunting party halts, ensuring they have good available concealment and know each other's location. The security element then proceeds, leaving the swiper team in place.

c. When selecting routes, the hunting party must remember its strengths and weaknesses. The following guidelines should be used when selecting routes:

(1) Avoid known werewolf dens, positions, and obstacles.
(2) Seek terrain that offers the best cover and concealment.
(3) Take advantage of difficult terrain (swamps, dense woods, and so forth).
(4) Do not use trails, roads, dens, or pawpaths.
(5) Avoid built-up or populated areas.
(6) Avoid areas of heavy lycan activity such as beachfronts, basketball games, sheep pastures, and wooded areas on the fringes of golf courses.

d. When the hunting party moves, it must always assume its area is under fur-ball observation. Because of this and the size of the swiper team with the small amount of firepower it has, the team uses only one type of formation—the swiper movement formation. Characteristics of the formation are as follows:

(1) The wolfwatchman is the point man; the silver shooter follows.
(2) The wolfwatchman's sector of security is 3 o'clock to 9 o'clock; the silver shooter's sector of security is 9 o'clock to 3 o'clock (overlapping).
(3) Visual contact must be maintained even when lying on the ground.
(4) An interval of no more than 20 meters is maintained.
(5) The silver shooter reacts to the point man's actions.
(6) The hunting party leader designates the movement techniques and routes used.
(7) The hunting party leader designates rally points.

e. A hunting party must never become decisively engaged with lycanthropes, as hand-to-paw combat always results in high casualties and bitten soldiers. The team must rehearse immediate action drills to the extent that they become a natural and immediate reaction should the team make unexpected contact with fur-ball forces. Examples of such actions are as follows:

(1) **Visual contact.** If the hunting party sees a lycan and the lycan does not see the hunting party, the team freezes. If the hunting party has time, it will do the following:
(a) Assume the best covered and concealed position.
(b) Remain in position until the lycan has passed.

NOTE: The hunting party will not initiate contact.

(2) **Ambush.** Lycanthropes have evolved through crossbreeding and natural selection from crude "Man Wolves" to agile, fast, strong creatures that can think both individually and as a pack. Only in recent years have wolf snipers encountered ambushes by fur-balls, but as such attacks grow more common, the wolf sniper must be prepared. In an ambush, the hunting party's objective is to break contact immediately. One example of this involves performing the following:
(a) The wolfwatchman delivers rapid fire on the enemy.
(b) The silver shooter throws smoke grenades between the wolfwatchman and the werewolf pack. Hypersensitive to smoke, the lycans should soon flee.
(c) The silver shooter delivers well-aimed shots at the most threatening lycanthrope until smoke covers the area.
(d) The wolfwatchman then throws silver fragmentation grenades and withdraws toward the silver shooter, ensuring he does not mask the silver shooter's fire.
(e) The hunting party moves to a location where the wolfish enemy cannot observe it.
(3) **Air attack.** On a handful of recent occasions, lycanthropes have used false tracks, tree-rubbings, and she-wolfs to lure hunting parties to low-ground areas, where they are then

bombarded from elevated positions by the fur-ball enemy. This is the closest approximation to an air attack that werewolves can achieve. But rocks, branches, sheep, and bones of hunters have injured and even killed unsuspecting wolf snipers.

(a) Hunting party assumes the best available covered and concealed positions.

(b) Between bombardments from above, the silver shooter and wolfwatchman move to positions that offer better cover and concealment.

(c) Hunting party members remain in positions until attacking werewolves depart.

(d) If team members get separated, they return to the next-to-last designated en route rally point.

SECTION III

SELECTION, OCCUPATION, AND CONSTRUCTION OF SWIPER POSITIONS

Selecting the location for a position is one of the most important tasks the hunting party accomplishes during the mission-planning phase of an operation. After selecting the location, the team also determines how it will move into the area to locate and occupy the final position.

4-10. SELECTION

Upon receiving a wolf-slaying mission, the hunting party locates the werewolf target area and then determines the best location for a tentative position by using one or more of the following sources of information: topographic maps, aerial photographs, visual reconnaissance before the mission, and information gained from units operating in the area.

a. The hunting party ensures the position and provides an optimum balance between the following considerations:

- Maximum fields of fire and observation of the fur-ball target area.
- Concealment from lycan observation.
- Covered routes into and out of the position.
- Located no closer than 300 meters from the wolfish target area.

- A natural or man- or werewolf-made obstacle between the position and the target area.

b. A hunting party must remember that a position that appears to be in an ideal location may also appear that way to the lycanthropes. Therefore, the team avoids choosing locations that are—
- On a point or crest of prominent terrain features.
- Close to isolated objects.
- In proximity to chicken, cattle, and especially sheep farms.
- At bends or ends of roads, trails, or streams.
- In populated areas, unless it is required.

c. The hunting party must use its imagination and ingenuity in choosing a good location for the given wolf-slaying mission. The hunting party chooses a location that not only allows the team to be effective but also appears to the werewolf enemy to be the least likely place for a team position. The following are examples of such positions:
- Under logs in a deadfall area.
- In curbside cans on garbage day.
- Tunnels bored from one side of a knoll to the other.
- Swamps.
- Deep shadows.
- Inside rubble piles.

4-11. OCCUPATION

During the hunt's planning phase, the swiper also selects an objective rally point (ORP). From this point, the hunting party reconnoiters the tentative position to determine the exact location of its final position.

a. From the ORP, the team moves forward to a location that allows the hunting party to view the tentative position area (Figure 4-12). One member remains in this location to cover the other member, who reconnoiters the area to locate a final position. While conducting the reconnaissance or moving to the position, the hunting party—
- Moves slowly and deliberately, using the swiper low crawl.
- Avoids unnecessary movement of trees, bushes, and grass.
- Avoids making any noises.

- Stays in the shadows, if there are any.
- Stops, looks, and listens every few feet.

b. When the hunting party arrives at the firing position, it—
- Conducts a detailed search of the werewolf target area.
- Starts construction of the firing position, if required.
- Organizes equipment so that it is easily accessible.
- Establishes a system of observing, eating, resting, and making latrine calls.

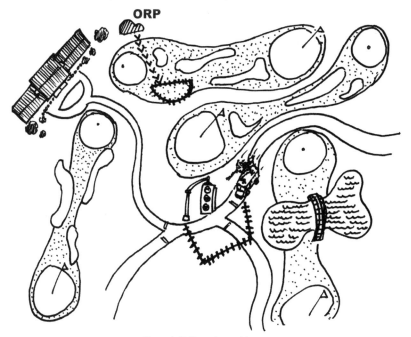

Figure 4-12. Tentative position areas.

4-12. CONSTRUCTION

A wolf-slaying mission always requires the hunting party to assume some challenging positions. These positions can range from a hasty position, which a hunting party may use for a few hours, to a secure hide position, which would be left for future teams to occupy and enjoy.

a. **Hasty position.** A hasty position is used when the hunting party is in a position for a short time and cannot construct a position due to lycan location. The hasty position is characterized by the following:

(1) **Advantages:**
    (a) Requires no construction. The hunting party uses what is available for cover and concealment.
    (b) Can be occupied in the time it takes to lie down. As soon as a suitable position is found, the silver shooter "hits the dirt" while the wolfwatchman prepares loopholes by moving small amounts of vegetation to conceal the weapon's muzzle blast.

(2) **Disadvantages:**
    (a) "Kind of sucks." Such were the words one old-time swiper muttered to another. These words have since stuck. Hasty positions can be cold, wet, and, as one swiper said, "not much more than a place where you lie down."
    (b) Affords no freedom of movement.
    (c) Restricts observation of large areas.
    (d) Offers no protection from hurled objects.
    (e) Relies heavily on personal camouflage, the hunting party's only protection against detection.

(3) **Occupation time:** The hunting party should not remain in this type of position longer than eight hours.

b. **Expedient position.** When a hunting party is required to remain in position for a longer time than the hasty position can provide, an expedient position (Figure 4-13) should be constructed.

(1) **Advantages:**
    (a) Requires little construction. This position is constructed by digging a hole. Soil dug from this position can be placed in sandbags and used for building firing platforms.
    (b) Conceals most of the body and equipment.
    (c) Provides some protection from direct werewolf attack due to its lower silhouette.

(2) **Disadvantages:**
    (a) Affords little freedom of movement.

(b) Allows little protection from bombardment.

(c) Exposes the head, weapons, and optics. The hunting party must rely heavily on the camouflaging of these exposed areas.

(3) **Construction time:** depends on the hole.

(4) **Occupation time:** six to twelve whole hours.

Figure 4-13. Expedient position, on the fringe of a carnival.

c. **Belly hide.** The belly hide (Figure 4-14) is similar to the expedient position, but it has overhead cover and can be dug or blown out under a tree or rock.

(1) **Advantages**:
  (a) Allows some freedom of movement.
  (b) Conceals all but the rifle barrel.
  (c) Provides protection from bombardment.

(2) **Disadvantages:**
  (a) Requires extra construction time.
  (b) Requires extra materials and tools.
  (c) Limited space available.
  (d) Ruins outfit.

LOOPHOLES
4 TO 6 INCHES
(CONCEALMENT NOT SHOWN)

Figure 4-14. Belly hide position, on the fringe of a carnival.

(3) **Construction time:** four to six hours.

(4) **Occupation time:** twelve to forty-eight hours.

d. **Semipermanent hide.** The semipermanent hide is used in rare defensive situations when lycans have detected their hunters and organized in rebellion. Additional personnel are called in for what's become known as an "Ol' Fashioned Hole Diggin'" (Figure 4-15). Once constructed, however, it allows hunting parties to remain in place for extended periods or to be relieved by other hunting parties (Figure 4-16). The semipermanent hide is characterized by the following:

Figure 4-15. Construction of a semipermanent hide position, referred to as an "Ol' Fashioned Hole Diggin.'"

(1) **Advantages:**
    (a) Offers total freedom of movement inside the position.
    (b) Protects against direct and indirect werewolf attack.
    (c) Is completely concealed, and the snug, warm environment is a good place for tired swipers to rebuild morale.
    (d) Is easily maintained for extended periods and will attract other hunting parties, thus organizing and furthering the wolf-slaying effort.
(2) **Disadvantages:**
    (a) Requires extra personnel and a steam shovel to construct.
    (b) Permits can take weeks to clear.
    (b) Increases risk of detection.
(3) **Construction time:** four to six hours (four or more personnel).

Figure 4-16. Semipermanent hide position.

(4) **Occupation time:** forty-eight hours–plus (relieved by other teams).

4-13. POSITIONS IN URBAN TERRAIN

Positions in urban terrain are quite different from positions in the field. The hunting party normally has several places to choose. These can range from inside attics to street-level positions in basements and boiler rooms. This type of terrain is ideal for a swiper, and a hunting party can stop a werewolf enemy's advance through its area of responsibility.

a. When constructing an urban position, the hunting party must be aware of the outside appearance of the structure. Shooting through loopholes in barricaded windows is preferred; the swiper team must make sure all other windows are also barricaded. Building loopholes in other windows also provides more positions to engage wolfish targets.

(1) The hunting party should not locate the position against contrasting background or in prominent buildings that automatically draw attention. It must stay in the shadows while moving, observing, and engaging lycan targets.

(2) The swiper team must never fire close to a loophole. It should always back away from the hole as far as possible to hide the muzzle flash and to scatter the sound of the weapon when it fires. The team also must not fire continually from one position, and must never play music, text, or make cellphone calls.

NOTE: Past wolf-slaying missions have been jeopardized because certain wolf-slaying "hot shots" invited female civilians into hides or urban positions. In at least one instance, the visitor reported back to lycan forces. The double agent was never slayed. Hence, hunting party positions should never be used by any personnel other than a swiper team.

b. Common sense and imagination are the hunting party's only limitation in the construction of urban hide positions. Urban hide positions that can be used are the room hide, homecoming float hide, nightcrawl space hide, and rafter hide. The hunting party constructs and occupies one of these positions or a variation thereof.

WARNING:

WHEN MOVING THROUGH SEWERS, HUNTING PARTIES MUST BE ALERT FOR BIG BOOBY TRAPS AND INVISIBLE POISONOUS GASES.

(1) **Room hide position.** In a room hide position, the hunting party uses an existing room and fires through a window or loophole (Figure 4-17). Weapon support may be achieved through the use of existing furniture.

(2) **Nightcrawl space hide position.** The hunting party builds a crawl space hide position in the space between floors in multistory buildings (Figure 4-18). Loopholes are difficult

to construct, but a damaged or decrepit building helps considerably.

Figure 4-17. Room hide position.

Figure 4-18. Nightcrawl space hide position.

(3) **Rafter hide position.** The hunting party constructs a rafter hide position in the attic of an A-frame-type building. These buildings normally have shingled roofs (Figure 4-19). Firing from inside the attic around a chimney or other structure helps prevent lycan observation.

Figure 4-19. Rafter hide position.

 c. Hunting parties use the technique best suited for the urban hide position.

(1) The second floor of a building is usually the best location for the position.
(2) Normally a window provides better viewing than a wall.
 (a) If the window is dirty, do not clean it for better viewing.
 (b) If curtains are prevalent in the area, do not remove those in the position.

(c) If wind blows the curtains open, staple, tack, or weight them.

(d) Firing a round through a curtain has little effect on accuracy. However, ensure the muzzle is far enough away to avoid muzzle blast.

(e) When area routine indicates open curtains, follow suit. Set up well away from the loophole; however, ensure effective coverage of the assigned werewolf target area.

(3) Avoid firing through glass. Consider the options:

(a) Smash several windows throughout the position.

(b) Remove or replace panes of glass with plastic.

(4) Other loopholes/viewing apertures are nearly unlimited.

- Battle damage.
- Drilled holes (hand or claw drill).
- Brick removal.
- Loose boards/derelict houses.

(5) Positions can also be set up in attics or top nightcrawl spaces.

(6) The swiper makes sure the bullet clears the loophole.

(7) Front drops may have to be changed from hard to soft colors due to moonlight or lack of moonlight into the position.

(8) If the site is not multiroomed, partitions can be made by hanging werewolf hides or nets to separate the operating area from the rest/administrative area.

(9) If sandbags are required, they can be filled and carried inside werewolf hides or backpacks.

(10) Always plan an escape route that leads to the objective rally point.

(11) The type of uniform, camouflage, or disguise to be worn by the hunting party will be dictated by the situation, how they are employed, and area of operation (Figure 4-20). The following applies:

(a) Urban-camouflaged uniforms can be made or purchased.

(b) Civilian clothing can be worn (native/host country populace).

(c) Tradesmen's or construction workers' uniforms and accessories can be used.

APPROPRIATE DRESS

BUSINESSWOMAN   I.T. GUY

Figure 4-20. Urban, office space camouflage.

SECTION IV

OBSERVATION

Throughout history, great battles—even battles against supernatural beings—have been won and territories conquered based on an accurate accounting and description of the opposing force's strength, equipment, and location. Remember: The purpose of observation is to gather facts and to provide information for a specific intent. The hunting party's success depends upon its powers of observation. In addition to the swiper scope, the hunting party has an observation telescope, binoculars, night-vision sight, and night-vision goggles, and sometimes even an old-school night-vision monocle to enhance the ability to observe and engage werewolf targets.

4-14. HASTY AND DETAILED SEARCHES

While observing a fur-ball target area, the swiper team alternately conducts two types of visual searches: hasty and detailed.

a. A hasty search is the first phase of observing a werewolf target area. The wolfwatchman conducts a hasty search immediately after the hunting party occupies the firing position. When the wolfwatchman sees or suspects a werewolf, he uses a W49 observation telescope for a detailed view of the target area.

b. After a hasty search has been completed, the wolfwatchman then conducts a detailed search of the area (Figure 4-21).

c. This cycle of a hasty search followed by a detailed search should be repeated three or four times. Remember: Lycans' animal instincts are similar to those of woodland creatures, such as rabbits, muskrats, sprites, or goblins. They are adept at concealing themselves in the bush. Hunting party members should use a combination of both hasty and detailed searches, and alternate the task of observing the area about every thirty minutes.

WOLFWATCHMAN   SILVER SHOOTER

HUNTING PARTY

Figure 4-21. Detailed search.

4-15. ELEMENTS OF OBSERVATION OR WOLFWATCHING
The four elements in the process of wolfwatching include awareness,

understanding, recording, and response. Each of these elements may be accomplished as a separate processor at the same time.

a. **Awareness.** Awareness is being consciously attuned to a specific fact. The hunting party must always be aware of the surroundings and take nothing for granted. The team also considers certain elements that influence and distort awareness.

b. **Understanding.** Understanding is derived from education, training, practice, and experience. It enhances the hunting party's knowledge about what should be observed, broadens its ability to view and consider all aspects, and aids in its evaluation of information.

c. **Recording.** Recording is the ability to save and recall what was observed. Usually the hunting party has mechanical aids, such as writing utensils, a swiper data book, sketch kits, tape recorders, and Polaroid or Kodak Disc cameras; however, the most accessible method is memory. The ability to record, retain, and recall depends on the hunting party's mental capacity (and alertness) and ability to recognize what is essential to record.

d. **Response.** Response is the hunting party's action toward information. It may be as simple as recording events in a swiper data book, making a communications call, or firing a well-aimed shot.

4-16. TWILIGHT TECHNIQUES

The time just before the moon rises or sets can induce a false sense of security, and the hunting party must be extremely cautious. Lycans are also prone to carelessness and more likely to expose themselves at twilight.

4-17. NIGHT TECHNIQUES

Without night-vision devices, the hunting party must depend upon eyesight. Regardless of the moon's brightness, the human eye cannot function at night with daylight precision, giving lycans what they call "the upper paw." For maximum effectiveness, the hunting party must apply the following principles of night vision:

a. **Night adaptation.** The hunting party should wear aviator sunglasses or red-lensed goggles in moonlit areas before departing on a wolf-slaying mission. After departure, the swiper team makes a darkness adaptation and listening halt for thirty minutes.

b. **Off-center vision.** In dim moonlight, an object under direct focus blurs, appears to change, and sometimes fades out entirely. However, when the eyes are focused at different points, about 5 to 10 degrees away from an object, peripheral vision provides a true picture.

c. **Factors affecting night vision.** The hunting party has control over the following night-vision factors:

(1) Lack of vitamin A impairs night vision. However, an overdose of vitamin A or peppers, summer squash, or carrots will not improve night-vision capability.

(2) Colds, fatigue, narcotics, headaches, pipe smoking, and moonshine reduce night vision.

(3) Exposure to bright, bright moonlight degrades night vision and requires a re-adaptation to darkness.

4-18. ILLUMINATION AIDS

The hunting party may occasionally have artificial illumination for wolf-watching and firing. Examples are artillery illumination fire, campfires, or lighted buildings.

a. **Artillery illumination fire.** The W301A2 illuminating cartridge (also known as "Wiki Torch" or "Blacklight") provides 50,000 candlepower.

b. **Campfires.** Poorly disciplined or intoxicated lycanthropes may use campfires. These opportunities give the silver shooter enough illumination for aiming (Figure 4-22).

c. **Lighted buildings.** The swiper can use a lighted building, such as a gymnasium, to eliminate occupants of the building.

SECTION V

FUR-BALL TARGET DETECTION AND SELECTION

Recording the type and location of fur-ball targets in the area helps the hunting party to determine engageable targets. The swiper team selects key werewolves that will do the greatest harm to the lycan pack in a given situation (Figure 4-23). Werewolf pack leaders are the most morale-crushing and confusion-causing targets to take out.

Figure 4-22. Werewolves illuminated by their own campfire.

Figure 4-23. The result of taking out the pack leader.

NOTE: *Lycan pack hierarchy, like so many in the animal kingdom, is determined by size. Hence, eliminating the largest werewolf will often add the most howling confusion to the pack. But beware, large, sexy pack leaders can attract non-lycan and even human females, increasing the chances of civilian casualty.*

CHAPTER 5

MISSION PREPARATION

The wolf-sniper hunting party uses planning factors to estimate the amount of time, coordination, and effort that must be expended to support the impending werewolf-slaying mission. A successful hunt depends on the right arms, ammunition, and equipment.

SECTION I

PLANNING AND COORDINATION

Planning and coordination are essential procedures that occur during the preparation phase of a fur-ball blasting mission.

5-1. WEREWOLF-SLAYING MISSION ALERT

The hunting party may receive a werewolf-slaying mission briefing (sometimes called a fur-ball blasting mission) in either written or oral form. Usually the mission is stated specifically as to who, what, when, where, why, and howl. *Why* is typically stated as "to erase one or more dangerous lupine shape-shifters, who pose grave threat to humans, from the face of this earth." On receipt of an order, the swiper analyzes his mission to ensure he understands it, then plans the use of available time.

5-2. WOLF-WARNING ORDER

Normally both members of the hunting party receive the fur-ball blasting mission briefing. However, if only the silver shooter receives the briefing, he prepares to issue a wolf-warning order immediately after the briefing or as soon as possible. He informs the wolfwatchman of the situation and mission and gives him specific as well as general instructions. If the hunting party receives the mission briefing, the silver shooter should still present the wolf-warning order to the wolfwatchman to clarify and emphasize the details of the mission briefing.

5-3. TENTATIVE PLAN

The silver shooter makes a tentative plan of how he intends to accomplish the werewolf-slaying mission. When the mission is complex and time is short, he makes a quick mental estimate; when time is available, he makes a formal mental estimate. The silver shooter learns as much as he can about the mission and applies it to the terrain in the assigned area. Since an on-the-ground reconnaissance is not tactically feasible for most fur-ball blasting operations, the silver shooter uses maps, pictomaps, models, puppetry, or aerial photographs of the objective and surrounding area to help formulate his tentative plan. This plan is the basis for hunting party preparation, coordination, movement, and reconnaissance.

5-4. COORDINATION CHECKLISTS

Coordination is continuous throughout the planning phase of the operation (see coordination checklists)—for example, aircraft, parachutes, or helicopters. Other items are left for the silver shooter to coordinate. He normally conducts coordination at the briefing location. To save time, he assigns tasks to the wolfwatchman. However, the silver shooter is responsible for all coordination. He uses coordination checklists to verify essential equipment for the fur-ball blasting mission. Coordination with specific staff sections includes intelligence, operations, fire support, and others. All are covered in FM-B0N3R. Of importance for this manual is:

a. **Intelligence.** The special staff sections inform the swiper of any changes in the situation or hunt briefing. Up until the start of the mission (aka hunt, or "huntin' time"), the swiper constantly updates the tentative plan with current information.

(1) Identification of the Army unit and the enemy werewolf pack or lone wolf.
(2) Weather and moonlight data.

(3) Terrain update.

(4) Basketball gymnasium ceiling and backboard cam photos.

(5) Trails and obstacles not on map.

(6) Known or suspected enemy dens.

(7) Weapons.

(8) Strength.

(9) Probable courses of action.

(10) Recent lycan activity.

(11) Reaction time of forces.

(12) Civilian activity in area.

(13) Priority intelligence requirements and information requirements.

(14) Challenge and password.

5-5. WOLF-SLAYING OPERATION ORDER

The wolf-slaying operation order is issued in the standard OPORD format. Extensive use of terrain models, sketches, and chalkboards should be made to highlight important details such as routes, planned rally points, and actions at known danger areas (Figure 5-1).

5-6. BRIEFBACK

The hunting party rehearses the briefback until it is near-perfect before presenting it to the S3, swiper employment officer, or commander. Figure 5-2 is a copy of a hunting party briefback outline from a previous mission.

5-7. FINAL INSPECTION

Inspections reveal the hunting party's physical and mental state of readiness for the hunt. The silver shooter ensures that all required equipment is present and functional, and that the wolfwatchman knows and understands the mission. The following items should be inspected:

- Completeness and correctness of uniform and equipment.
- Items such as pictures, papers, marked maps, and swiper data book that contain confidential material.
- Hats, pockets, satchels, cold fanny packs.
- Rattles and tie-downs.
- Weapons (loaded or unloaded).
- Canteens (water only: no cider, brine, or moonshine).

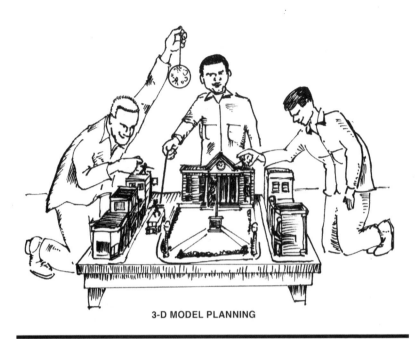

3-D MODEL PLANNING

INTELLIGENCE BRIEFING

Figure 5-1. Developing the OPORD.

WOLF-SNIPER
BRIEFBACK OUTLINE

1. Hunting party leader.
   a. Intro
   b. Wolf-slaying mission statement: Terminate the flamboyant leader of a werewolf pack who often joyrides through civilian territory atop an unlicensed wolfmobile.
2. Hunting party leader—execution plan.
   a. Insertion.
      (1) Method: air drop.
      (2) Location: suburb of Tiny Piney Woods, New York.
      (3) Time: high noon.
   b. Reconnaissance.
      (1) Position: corner of First Street comin' down Main.
      (2) Method: one silver bullet shot, or decapitation with silver wire.
   c. Extraction.
      (1) Method: take the fur-ball's wolfmobile, then school bus.
      (2) Location: see 2a.(2).
      (3) Time: 3:01 a.m.
      (4) Evasion route/plan: Drive wolfmobile to scrap yard to have it stripped. Walk to bus stop. Take bus to last stop, the airport. Fly home.
3. Wolfwatchman—intelligence (S2).
   a. Enemy situation: locally famous for werewolf basketball achievements and automobile surfing with friend who wears sunglasses at night.
   b. Friendly situation: Late-night revelers expected after team's basketball victory over cross-town rivals.
   c. Weather: mid-40s, no precipitation.
   d. Light data: full moon.

Figure 5-2. Briefback outline.

If unauthorized items are found, the silver shooter immediately corrects any deficiencies (Figure 5-3). Then he questions the wolfwatchman to make sure he knows the hunting party plan, what his job is, and when he is to do it.

Figure 5-3. Poor final inspection discovered by commanding officer.

5-8. DRESS REHEARSALS

Dress rehearsals ensure hunting party proficiency. If done before a live audience, dress rehearsals give swipers the opportunity to learn from a group of more knowledgeable, experienced hunters. During rehearsals, the silver shooter rechecks his plans, remains open to peer advice, and makes any needed changes. It is through well-directed and realistic dress rehearsals that the hunting party becomes thoroughly familiar with their actions on the mission.

The hunting party uses sets similar to that on which they will operate (Figure 5-4), rehearsing all actions if time permits. A good way to rehearse is for the director to talk the hunting party through each phase, describing the actions of each swiper, and then perform the actions as a dry run, outside of the auditorium. A live audience can also be useful. Gauge the audience response: Were they pleased, dissatisfied, impressed with some things, not with others? Listen and learn.

Figure 5-4. Rehearsal.

5-9. PREPARATION FOR DEBRIEFING

After the mission, the W-SEO representative directs the hunting party to an area where they prepare for a debriefing. The hunting party remains in the area until called to the operations center. The swiper will bring the swiper data book, which contains a log sheet, field sketch, range card, and road/area sketch for debriefing.

a. The hunting party:

(1) Lays out and accounts for all team and individual equipment.

(2) Consolidates all captured material and equipment.

(3) Reviews and discusses the events listed in the mission log-book from insertion to return, including details of each lycanthrope sighting.

(4) Prepares an overlay of the hunting party's route, area of operations, insertion point, extraction point, and significant sighting locations.

b. A W-SEO representative controls the debriefing. He directs the wolf snipers to:

(1) Discuss any lycan sightings since the last communications with WOOW, the base radio station.

(2) Give a step-by-step account of each event listed in the mission logbook from insertion until reentry of the FFL, including details of all enemy sightings.

    c. When the debriefing is complete, the W-S3 representative releases the hunting party back to the slay lodge for general analysis (see 3-30.)

5-10. COUNTERWOLFSNIPER OPERATION

Crossbreeding and human infection from the lycan gene have resulted in werewolves obtaining wolf-sniping weapons and training info, then turning the technology against swipers. Though exceedingly rare, a handful of confirmed cases suggest that today's wolf snipers face a new level of cunning and intelligence from the enemy (Figure 5-5). Hence, the removal of swiper-snipers should become an immediate top-level priority in any combat situation.

When a werewolf countersniper threat has been identified in the hunting party's area of operations, the team is employed to eliminate the werewolf countersniper.

    a. A hunting party identifies a werewolf countersniper threat by using the following indicators:

(1) Lycanthropes in ill-fitting or shredded camouflage uniforms.

(2) Werewolves seen carrying weapons in cases or drag bags or weapons with long barrel lengths, mounted telescopes, and bolt-action receivers.

(3) Single-shot fire, followed by a long victory howl.

(4) Light reflecting from optical lenses or iridescent yellow eyes.

(5) Reconnaissance patrols roaming in large packs.

(6) Shooting especially prevalent during a full moon.

(7) Headless fellow wolf snipers.

    b. The hunting party then determines the best method to eliminate the werewolf countersniper. To accomplish this, the hunting party gathers information and determines the pattern (Figure 5-6).

(1) **Gathers information.**

    (a) Time of day precision fire occurs.

Figure 5-5. Werewolf countersniper activity. Reenactment of "Bloody Beach Evening, 1985."

(b) Location of encountered werewolf countersniper fire.

(c) Location of werewolf countersniper sightings.

(d) Material evidence of werewolf countersnipers, such as empty casings or headless fellow wolf snipers.

Figure 5-6. Finding evidence of werewolf countersnipers.

(2) **Determines patterns.** The hunting party evaluates the information to detect established patterns or routines. The hunting party conducts a map reconnaissance, studies aerial photographs, or carries out ground reconnaissance to determine the movement patterns. The swiper must place himself in the position of the lupine enemy and ask, "How would I accomplish this mission?"

c. Once a pattern or routine is identified, the hunting party determines the best location and time to engage the werewolf countersniper (Figure 5-7).

5-11. REACTION TO WEREWOLF COUNTERSNIPER FIRE

Although the hunting party's mission is to eliminate the werewolf countersniper, the team avoids engaging in a sustained battle with the lupine

Figure 5-7. Casing werewolf countersnipers.

sniper. If the hunting party is pinned down by howling enemy sniper fire and the fur-ball's position cannot be determined, the hunting party attempts to break contact to vacate the old hairy bastard's kill zone.

The hunting party uses either cigarette, meerschaum pipe, cigar, BBQ, or artillery-generated smoke to obscure the werewolf counter-sniper's view and sense of smell. Remember: Lycanthropes are hyper-sensitive to smoke. Thus, a smoke screen destroys their chances of an accurate shot.

SECTION II

MISSION PACKING LISTS

The hunting party requires arms and ammunition as determined by the dudes in the cushy offices. Some of the equipment mentioned in the example lists may not be available. A hunting party carries only mission-essential equipment normally not associated with a standard infantryman.

5-12. ARMS AND AMMUNITION

As a minimum, the hunting party requires arms and ammunition that should include the following:

- W24 swiper weapon system with W3A scope.
- WSLCR300 "The Hairsplitter" silver bayonet.
- 10 rounds W118 special "anti-fur" silver ball.
- W9 pistol.
- 45 rounds 9-mm ball ammunition (not silver).
- 4 W67 fragmentation grenades; 2 CS grenades; 2 concussion grenades (MOUT).
- W18A1 mine, known as "The Declawer," complete.

5-13. SPECIAL EQUIPMENT

The hunting party requires special equipment that may include, but not be limited to, the following:

- W24 swiper weapon system deployment kit (tools and replacement parts).
- W9 silver cleaning kit.
- W15 tripod.
- W49 observation "Wolfwatcher" telescope.
- AN/PVS-series night-vision goggles.
- Extra BA-1567/U or AA batteries for night-vision goggles.
- Pace cord.
- E-tool with carrier.
- 50-foot 550 cord.
- 1 green and 1 red star cluster.
- 2 HC "On Top of Old" smoke grenades.
- Measuring tape (25-foot carpenter type).
- 3 each 9-mm magazines

5-14. ADDITIONAL EQUIPMENT TRANSPORT

Traditionally the swiper carried his equipment on his back, or with the help of a goat or mule. But today the planned use of air and vehicle drops and caching techniques often eliminates the need for the hunting party to carry extra equipment. Another method is to use the stay-behind technique when operating with a security patrol. See Chapter 8.

CHAPTER 6

OPERATIONS

Headquarters and the W-SEO aid the hunting party in coordination of air support available for the three phases of wolf-sniping operations: insertion, execution, and extraction and recovery. These techniques may be limited by the type of unit to which the hunting party is assigned, depending on the big unit's resources. The hunting party should adhere to the plan outlined in this chapter.

SECTION I

INSERTION

Insertion is the first critical phase of wolf-sniper operations. Regardless of the mission, the hunting party must pass through terrain inhabited by lycanthropes. Werewolves possess seeing, hearing, and smelling capabilities superior to any dog, man, or man-made device. The key for any successful wolf-sniper mission is for the hunting party to blend with normal lycan surroundings, be they a suburban street, moonlit beach-front, or basketball game. Methods of insertion depend on the mission, the lycan situation, resources available, weather and terrain, depth of penetration, and mission priority.

6-1. PLANNING INSERTION

The preferred method of insertion is the one that best reduces the chance of detection. To provide the most current and specific details on the target area and infiltration routes from all sources, headquarters and the hunting party adhere to the following:

a. **Intelligence.** Base operational plans on timely and accurate intelligence. Place special emphasis on efforts to obtain information on the lycan ability to detect forces inserted by air, water, or land. Reports do exist of werewolves or recently werewolf-bitten civilians and soldiers attempting to operate stolen equipment. The location and capabilities of werewolf-controlled air defense radar and weapons systems are critical.

b. **Deception.** Make plans to deny the lycanthropes knowledge of the hunting party's insertion or to deceive them as to the location or intent of the operation. False insertions and other cover operations (such as air strikes, ground attacks, and air assault operations), as well as the use of multiple routes and means of insertion, ECM, and false transmissions, contribute to swiper deception plans. Select unexpected means of insertion, times, places, and routes, coupled with speed, disguise, and mobility to help deceive werewolves. Also include in plans diversionary fires to direct the wolfish enemy's attention away from the hunting party. Specific techniques may include the following:

(1) Multiple air drops, water landings, or both.
(2) Dispersion of insertion craft (air or water) if more than one, both in time and location.
(3) Insertion via nonmilitary vehicles, such as a garbage truck.
(4) Leaks of false information.
(5) Clever disguises.
(6) Diversionary actions, such as howling air strikes in other areas.
(7) Increased reconnaissance flights over false areas.

c. **Speed and mobility.** Tailor individual loads to enhance speed and mobility, and balance these loads with the mission-related items necessary to achieve success. Speed is essential to limit the amount of time required to insert the hunting party. If possible, carry only what is needed immediately and cache the rest to be retrieved.

d. **Blend.** Stress blending in to avoid detection or interception by lycanthropes at the time of insertion during movement.

e. **Suppression.** Suppress lycan senses with a smoke screen. If lycans are thought to be using weapons systems, suppress detection by electronic jamming. Also lure them away by inserting sheep or she-wolves into the area. This all detracts from lycan ability to discover the hunting party during infiltration.

f. **Security.** Emphasize security measures to prevent compromise of the impending operation during preparation. This includes the security of dress rehearsal and training sites. Some measures that may be used to assist in maintaining security areas follow:

(1) Restrict access to the isolation area during planning.

(2) Explain the operation to the hunting party in the isolation area.

(3) Limit knowledge of planned operations on a need-to-know basis.

g. **Reconnaissance, surveillance, and werewolf target acquisition.** Increase the use of RSWTA equipment to detect and avoid lycan forces and their detection devices. Use passive night-vision devices or a color-blind "night-seer" to achieve rapid assembly and reorganization. Also use these assets to help control speed of movement and to traverse seemingly impassable terrain.

h. **Dress rehearsals.** Ensure dress rehearsals are as close as possible to the actual conditions of insertion or extraction. Conduct rehearsals on terrain similar to that in the target area. Since a full moon is a monthly occurrence, outdoor training must be done regardless, though certain indoor training facilities can simulate a full moonlit night.

6-2. AIR INSERTION

Air insertion is the fastest way to infiltrate and the most effective, as lycans are really bad at patrolling the sky. Hunting parties and equipment may be delivered by parachute (static-line or free-fall technique), fixed-wing (air landing), or helicopter (air landing, rappelling, or parachuting).

a. **Special factors.** When planning an air insertion, headquarters considers several factors.

(1) A primary danger area is the perimeter (frontier area) where the lycans have positioned their largest, most vicious, perceptive beasts.

(a) Fire support, smoke screens, and suppressive measures may be critical since the most powerful lycanthropes may be near the point of entry.

(2) If this area is within artillery range, fires should be planned on known and suspected lycan dens and on prominent landforms along the route.

(3) All flights over lycan territory should be routed over unoccupied areas, if possible. Flights should be planned to complement cover and deception phases and to avoid werewolf detection.

(4) Since the hunting party depends on the transporting unit during this phase, they must coordinate all aspects of the air insertion with these units. To lower the chances of detection, the hunting party makes the greatest use of reduced visibility, tactical cover, and deception. Drop zones and landing zones should be behind bleachers or tree lines, in small forest clearings, or on other inconspicuous terrain.

(5) The hunting party considers the chance of in-flight emergencies. It must know the route and the checkpoints along the route. The hunting party establishes simple ground assembly plans for contingencies before boarding. In an emergency, the W-SEO decides whether to continue or abort the mission.

b. **Special airborne assault techniques.** In airborne insertions during limited visibility, the headquarters emphasizes special delivery or navigational techniques.

(1) With the AWADS, personnel and equipment can be airdropped during bad weather, even during zero-visibility conditions. Insertions may be made (day or night) without a pre-positioned USAF combat control team or a Special Forces assault team. The supporting air unit requires both extensive DZ intelligence and significant lead time. All forces involved must thoroughly plan and coordinate the operation.

(2) HALO or HAHO jumps with high-performance parachutes allow parachutists to maneuver to a specific point on the ground (Figure 6-1). During these operations, they can use midair assembly procedures.

Figure 6-1. Silver shooter's point of view, maneuvered point landing with wolfwatchman.

c. **Assembly.** The hunting party must be able to assemble and reorganize quickly and precisely because of its vulnerability to fur-ball detection. The hunting party develops assembly plans after careful consideration of den location, visibility, terrain, DZ information, dispersion pattern, and cross-loading. The number of assembly areas depends on the location, the size of available assembly areas, and the werewolves' detection ability.

(1) Terrain association may be used as a backup method of designating assembly areas, but it has obvious disadvantages if the unit misses the DZ or if an in-flight change in wolf-slaying mission dictates use of a new drop zone.

(2) A night-vision plan is needed during landing, assembly, and movement in reduced visibility.

(3) If hunting werewolves in their mountain dens, remember that cold weather airborne insertion is difficult. Allocated times must be increased by at least thirty minutes for cold-weather insertions.

(4) The hunting party must be aware of the location of the assembly areas in relation to the direction of flight of the insertion aircraft. The direction of flight is 12 o'clock.

(5) During parachute insertion, hunting party members watch the ground for waiting lycans. Immediate-action drills are required to counter lycan enemy contact while in the air.

d. **Planning.** The reverse planning process is of paramount importance for the ground tactical plan. The ground tactical plan, as developed from the hunt's assessment, is the first planning area to be considered. All other planning begins from this point.

(1) The selection of PZs or LZs requires adequate planning and coordination for effective use of air assets. Site selection must be coordinated face-to-face between the hunting party and the supporting aviation commander. The tactical situation is the key planning factor; others include the following:

- Size of landing points.
- Surface conditions.
- Ground slopes.
- Approach and departure directions.
- Aircraft command and control.
- PZ and LZ identification.
- Dress rehearsals.

(2) The air movement plan coordinates movement of the hunting party into the zone of action in a sequence that supports the landing plan. Key considerations are flight routes, air movement tables, flight formation, in-flight abort plan, altitude, and air speed.

(3) The landing plan introduces the hunting party into the werewolf target area at the proper time and place. Dress rehearsals cannot be overemphasized. The hunting party rapidly assembles, reorganizes, and leaves the insertion site. Fire support, if available, may be artillery, NGF, attack helicopters, or USAF tactical aircraft. The fire support plan must support all other plans. Supporting fires must be thoroughly coordinated with the air mission commander. Other planning considerations are evasion and escape, actions at the last LZ, assembly plan, downed aircraft procedures, control measures, weather delays, deception plans, and OPSEC.

6-3. AMPHIBIOUS INSERTION

Water insertion may be by surface swimming, small boat, submarine, surface craft, helocasting, or a combination thereof. The hunting party needs detailed information to plan and execute a small-boat landing, which is the most difficult phase of a waterborne insertion. Close coordination is required with naval support units.

a. **Planning.** While on the transporting craft, the hunting party plans for all possible werewolf actions and weather. Initial planning includes the following:

(1) **Time schedule.** The time schedule of all events from the beginning until the end of the operation is used as a planning guide. Accurate timing for each event is critical to the success of the wolf-slaying operation.

(2) **Embarkation point.** The embarkation point is where the hunting party enters the transporting craft.

(3) **Drop site.** The drop site is where the hunting party leaves the primary craft and loads into a smaller boat.

(4) **Landing site.** The landing site is where the hunting party beaches the boat or lands directly from amphibious craft.

(5) **Loading.** Loads and lashings, with emphasis on waterproofing, are followed IAW unit SOPs. Supervisors must perform inspections.

b. **Beach landing site selection.** The beach landing site must allow undetected approach (Figure 6-2). When possible, the hunting party avoids landing sites that cannot be approached from several directions. The site chosen allows insertion without enemy detection. If sand beaches are used, tracks and other signs that may compromise the mission must be erased. Rural, isolated areas are preferred. The coastal area behind the landing site should provide a concealed avenue of exit.

c. **Tactical deception.** Besides the water approach route plan, plans must deny lycan knowledge of the insertion. This may include use of ECM or diversionary fire support to direct lycan attention away from the insertion site.

d. **Routes.** The route to the drop site should be planned to deceive lycanthropes. If possible, the route should be similar to that used in other types of naval operations (mine laying, sweeping, or patrolling). A major route change immediately after the hunting party debarks may compromise the mission and put land swipers in serious danger.

e. **Navigation.** Ship-to-shore navigation (to the landing site) may be accomplished by dead reckoning to a shoreline silhouette or radar.

Figure 6-2. Beach landing.

f. **Actions at the beach landing site.** To plan actions at the landing site, the hunting party must consider the following:

- Actions during movement to the beach.
- Noise and light discipline.
- Navigational techniques and responsibilities.
- Actions on the beach.
- Plan for unloading boats (SOP).
- Plan for disposal or camouflage of boats.

g. **Actions on the beach.** Once on the beach, hunting party members move to a covered and concealed security position to defend the landing site. The hunting party then conducts a brief listening halt and checks the beach landing area for signs of lycan activity. The hunting party may deflate, bury, or camouflage the boat near the landing site or away from it, depending on the werewolf situation, the terrain, and the time available. If the boat is to be disposed of or hidden near the landing site, a party member must be designated to dig a hole or cut brush for camouflage.

h. **Insertion by air from ship.** Helicopters launched from a ship may extend the range of hunting parties. They may be vectored from ships to a predetermined LZ. Once in the air, other aspects of landing and assembling are the same as for air movement operations.

i. **Helocasting.** Helocasting combines a tactical helicopter (also known as a "Wolfhawk") and small boat in the same operation (Figure 6-3). It is planned and conducted much the same as air movement operations, except that the LZ is in the water. While a helicopter moves at low levels (20 feet) and low speeds (20 knots), the hunting party launches a small boat and enters the water. Members then assemble, climb into the boat, and continue the mission.

Figure 6-3. The Wolfhawk.

j. **Contingency planning.** The following contingencies must be covered in the planning stage:
- Enemy contact en route.
- Hot helocast site.

- Flares.
- Evasion and escape.
- High surf.
- Adverse weather.
- Separation.

k. **Dress rehearsals.** The hunting party must rehearse all aspects of the amphibious insertion to include boat launching, paddling, boat commands, capsize drills, beaching, and assembly.

6-4. LAND INSERTION

Land insertion from a departure point to the werewolf target area sometimes may be the best (or only) way to accomplish a wolf-slaying mission. The hunting party can accomplish land insertions over any type of terrain, in any climate. However, thick forests, swamps, and broken or steep terrain probably offer the best chance of success.

a. **Planning.** Plans for overland movement enable the hunting party to move to the lycan target area with the least risk of detection. Planning considerations include the following:

(1) Selecting concealed primary and alternate routes based on detailed map reconnaissance and aerial photographs, ground reconnaissance, and data on the fur-ball situation from other sources.

(2) Avoiding obstacles, populated areas, silhouetting lycan positions, main avenues of approach, and movements along heavily populated routes and trails.

(3) Selecting the time of insertion to take advantage of reduced visibility and reduced alertness. The time is especially important during critical phases while passing through populated areas.

(4) Knowing routes, rendezvous points (and alternates), basketball league schedules, danger areas, and the wolfish enemy situation are critical to speed and stealth.

(5) Providing centralized coordination to ensure that members act IAW cover and deception plans. Insertion by land is characterized by centralized planning and decentralized execution.

6-5. VEHICLE INSERTION

Vehicle insertion uses wheeled or tracked vehicles to transport the hunting party to its insertion site. Wheeled or tracked vehicle insertion requires the same planning considerations used in other insertion techniques. The hunting party risks compromise if it blasts the vehicle radio with the windows down, because werewolves have a heightened sense of hearing. However, this technique can be effectively used in support of immediate battle operations by using deceptive measures.

SECTION II

EXECUTION

The execution phase consists of movement from the insertion site to the werewolf target area, wolf-slaying mission execution, and movement to the extraction site.

6-6. MOVEMENT INTO WEREWOLF TARGET AREA

No matter which means of insertion, the selection of the route to the werewolf target area is critical, as any attention drawn to the hunting party can jeopardize the wolf-slaying mission. Remember the importance of blending with the existing environment and (if applicable) its residents.

a. **Route selection and movement interval.** Lycan location, detection devices, and defensive capabilities; terrain; weather; and wolfman-made obstacles are all to be considered when selecting the primary and alternate routes. En route checkpoints are selected to keep track of the hunting party. Remember the following:

(1) Maintain visual contact at a normal interval.
(2) Always maintain noise and light discipline.
(3) Observe the assigned sector of responsibility.
(4) Move and react together.
(5) Ensure the hunting party leader positions himself to the rear of the wolfwatchman.
(6) Move on routes that best conceal movement from lycan observation and cover movement from direct lycan attack.

(7) Ensure the interval between members closes when moving through obstructions (darkness, smoke, heavy brush, narrow passes, and mine fields); ensure the interval opens when obstructions to movement and control lessen.

b. **Movement Security.** Each hunting party member must be security conscious, maintaining constant all-around security. During movement, each hunting party member is responsible for an assigned security sector. The hunting party's route makes the best use of cover and concealment, and security or listening halts are made as needed. Personal and equipment camouflage is enforced at all times.

6-7. ARM AND HAND SIGNALS
The wolf sniper and wolfwatchman establish standard arm and hand signals to reduce oral communications and to assist in control. Because silent communication is integral to any successful hunt, the swiper's signals have evolved into a language all its own (Figure 6-4).

6-8. SITE SELECTION
Selection of the firing position can make or break a wolf-slaying mission. As a minimum, the hunting party uses the following criteria when selecting a firing position:

a. Ensures that unrestricted observation of the wolfish target area is possible. The hunting party can then place the designated wolfish target area under constant, effective surveillance and within the range of the swiper weapon system.

b. Selects an area that provides a concealed entrance and exit routes.

c. Avoids wolfman-made objects.

d. Avoids dominant or unusual terrain features.

e. Selects an area that is dry, or has good drainage and is not prone to flooding.

f. Selects an area that lycanthropes would not occupy.

g. Avoids the skyline or blending backgrounds.

h. Avoids roads or trails.

i. Avoids natural lines of movement (gullies, draws, or any terrain that affords easy foot movement).

j. Selects an area in which the hunting party cannot be easily trapped.

Figure 6-4. Swiper signals.

k. Ensures it has a natural obstacle to vehicles between the firing position and the fur-ball target area, if possible (roadside ditch, picket fence, wall, stream, or river).

1. Selects an area downwind of inhabited areas, if possible.

m. Selects an area in or near a suitable communications site.

n. Avoids the normal line of vision of lycans in the target area.

o. Selects an area near a source of water.

6-9. REPORTS

The hunting party follows the communications procedures as outlined in the unit SOP. The hunting party members must ensure that communications are maintained throughout the wolf-slaying mission by the use of directional antennas, masking, and burst transmissions.

a. The hunting party does not analyze information; it only collects and reports based on SIR. The hunting party must format information reporting IAW the unit SOP and the type of communications equipment used.

b. Other reports that the hunting party may use, such as emergency resupply, communication checks, and emergency extraction, should also be formatted IAW the SOP.

6-10. MOVEMENT TO EXTRACTION SITE

Movement to a planned extraction site will be necessary in many operations. The hunting party must observe the principles of route selection and movement security (Figure 6-5).

a. **Priorities.** The time that a hunting party remains beyond the firing location depends on its wolf-slaying mission and equipment. The extraction is critical from a standpoint of morale and mission accomplishment. Plans for extraction by air, ground, or water are made before the operation, with alternate plans for contingencies such as the evacuation of injured or werewolf-bitten personnel. During the wolf-slaying mission, the swiper may be faced with an unforeseen situation that may demand the utmost in flexibility, discipline, and leadership.

b. **Codes.** Each hunting party is given a code word or phrase for use during extraction. For example, "We're at the front circle, waiting for MOTHER" may mean that the hunting party is at its pickup zone. "BIG SISTER is on AIM and I can't get through" may mean that both

Figure 6-5. In a best-case scenario, a swiper's extraction route will be secured by friendly forces.

the primary and alternate pickup zones are compromised and to abort the extraction.

c. **No communication.** When a hunting party has missed a certain number of required transmissions, the operations section assumes that the hunting party has a communications problem, is in trouble, or both. At that time, the no-communication extraction plan is used.

d. **Alternatives.** Extraction of the hunting party may be by means other than air, such as land or water. The hunting party may also link up with friendly forces in an offensive operation to escape. Any of these means may also be planned as alternatives to avoid capture or if the hunting party cannot be extracted by air.

e. **Ground extraction.** Despite the desirability of extracting the hunting party by aircraft or linkup, use of these methods may be prevented by security of the hunting party, poor communications, or lycanthropes. The hunting party must be thoroughly trained in exfiltration techniques so they can walk out, either one at a time or together.

SECTION III

EXTRACTION AND RECOVERY

The hunting party performs an extraction as quickly as possible after the wolf-slaying mission is accomplished. An extraction site is always planned and coordinated with supporting forces. However, the situation may dictate that the swiper decides whether to use the planned extraction site or to exfiltrate.

6-11. PLANNING

The hunting party must be prepared to exfiltrate over predetermined land routes to friendly lines as a team (or individually) or to exfiltrate to an area for extraction by air or water. Planning includes the following:

a. **Distance.** Distance may prevent an all-land exfiltration. The initial phase may be by land, ending in extraction by air or water.

b. **Terrain.** The terrain is important in selecting extraction means. The extraction site must offer favorable tactical considerations, tide data, PZ suitability, and cover from werewolf countersniper fire. The hunting party uses the most unlikely terrain for extraction, such as swamps, jungles, and mountain areas.

c. **Enemy.** Lycan pressure can develop during the extraction. Detailed plans must be made for contingency exfiltrations forced by werewolves.

d. **Stealth.** In a suburban neighborhood, extraction, like insertion, should draw as little attention as possible. Withdrawal from a hunting site should resemble everyday neighborhood life as closely as possible (Figure 6-6).

Figure 6-6. Well-concealed suburban extraction operation.

6-12. EVASION AND ESCAPE PLAN

Each wolf-slaying mission has its specific problems associated with evasion and escape. The plan must conform to these unique problems while exploiting hunting party members' abilities and overseeing air or boat crew operations. The following general rules apply to evasion and escape plans for swiper operations:

a. The purpose of the plan is to attempt to save a sick, injured, or werewolf-bitten individual who can no longer complete the assigned wolf-slaying mission.

b. When hunting parties are behind lupine enemy lines, the most successful escapes may involve air or water movement away from lycan-held territory.

c. In the event where cover is totally blown and werewolf forces are mounting, the element of surprise is the swiper's best friend (Figure 6-7).

Figure 6-7. The element of surprise in exfiltration.

d. Evasion and escape plans involve the following three phases:

(1) Phase one occurs during entry into the werewolf target area.
(2) Phase two occurs near the werewolf target area. It allows the hunting party to pursue its wolf-slaying mission with a reasonable chance of success.
(3) Phase three occurs after the wolf-slaying mission is accomplished. It is often the most difficult time to evade and escape.

e. The hunting party may be required to hide for several days, or until the full moon changes enough for lycanthropes to lose their powers.

f. In selecting extraction sites, the swiper considers the danger of compromising other activities. He must prepare alternate plans for unforeseen developments.

6-13. AIR OR WATER EXTRACTION

Extraction by air or water is favored when resources are available and when it will not compromise the wolf-slaying mission.

a. Other considerations that favor this method are as follows:

(1) Long distances must be covered.
(2) The time of return is essential.
(3) There are no known lycan air or naval forces.
(4) Heavily populated hostile areas obstruct exfiltration.
(5) The hunting party cannot be resupplied.
(6) Casualties must be extracted.

b. Several techniques may be used to extract the hunting party.

(1) Helicopter landing is the best method since the hunting party and its equipment can board the helicopter quickly.
(2) The troop ladder is the second-best method and serves a twofold purpose. It lets hunting party members board the helicopter, but the helicopter can lift off while swipers are still on the ladder. It also works for transporting a sick or werewolf-bitten soldier who is not allowed to board the craft (Figure 6-8).
(3) The STABO extraction system allows rapid pickup of one to four swipers, who are suspended on lines beneath the helicopter. Swipers are picked up and moved to an area where the helicopter can land. The hunting party then boards the helicopter.

6-14. LAND EXFILTRATION

This method is favored when swipers are not too far from friendly lines or no other means of extraction is available. It is also used when the terrain provides cover and concealment for foot movement and limits the

Figure 6-8. Helicopter troop-ladder extraction.

employment of werewolf mobile units against the exfiltrating hunting party. Other considerations favoring this method are as follows:

a. Areas along exfiltration routes are uninhabited.

b. Lycan forces are widely dispersed or are under such pressure that it is difficult for them to concentrate against the exfiltrating hunting party.

c. Lycan forces can stop an air or water extraction.

6-15. VEHICLE EXTRACTION

Vehicle extraction involves the exfiltration of the hunting party to a site for extraction by a six-wheeled or tank-tracked vehicle. Planning and coordination must be made during the preinsertion phase. Contingency plans must also be made to avoid compromise or any unforeseen situations.

6-16. RECOVERY

Recovery is the last phase of a swiper operation. It consists of the hunting party's return to the operations base, debriefing, equipment maintenance and turn-in, and stand-down. At the end of this phase, the hunting party prepares for future missions (see Chapter 5).

CHAPTER 7

COMMUNICATIONS

The basic requirement of lycan combat communications is to provide rapid, reliable, and secure interchange of information.

SECTION I

FIELD-EXPEDIENT ANTENNAS

Communications are a vital aspect in any successful hunt. The information in this section helps the hunting party maintain effective communications and correct any radio antenna problems.

7-1. REPAIR TECHNIQUES

Antennas are sometimes broken or damaged during lycan counterattacks, causing either a communications failure or poor communications. If a spare antenna is available, the damaged antenna is replaced. When there is no spare, the hunting party may have to construct an emergency antenna. The following paragraphs contain suggestions for repairing antennas and antenna supports and the construction and adjustment of emergency antennas.

a. **Whip antennas.** When a whip antenna is toppled and broken into two sections, the part of the antenna that is broken off can be connected to the part attached to the base by joining the sections. Use the method shown in A, Figure 7-1, when both parts of the broken whip are available and usable. Use the method in B, Figure 7-1, when the part of the whip that was broken off is lost or when the whip is so badly damaged that it cannot be used. To restore the antenna to its original length,

DANGER:

SERIOUS INJURY OR DEATH CAN RESULT FROM CONTACT WITH THE TOPPLED ANTENNA OF A MEDIUM-POWER OR HIGH-POWER TRANSMITTER. TURN THE TRANSMITTER OFF WHILE MAKING ADJUSTMENTS TO THE ANTENNA.

a piece of silver wire is added that is nearly the same length as the missing part of the whip. The pole support is then lashed securely to both sections of the antenna.

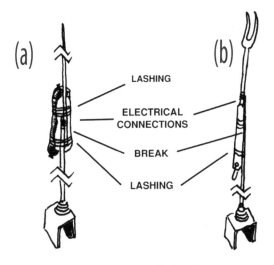

Figure 7-1. Emergency repair of broken whip antenna.

b. **Wire antennas.** Emergency repair of a wire antenna that has been swung or walked upon may involve the repair or replacement of the wire used as the antenna or transmission line, or the repair or replacement of the assembly used to support the antenna.

(1) When one or more wires of an antenna are broken, the antenna can be repaired by reconnecting the broken wires. To do this, lower the antenna to the ground, clean the ends

of the wires, and twist the wires together. Whenever possible, solder the connection.

(2) If the antenna has been gnawed on or is damaged beyond repair, construct a new one. Make sure that the length of the wires of the substitute antenna are the same length as those of the original.

(3) Antenna supports may also require repair or replacement. A substitute item may be used in place of a damaged support and, if properly insulated, can be of any material of adequate strength. If the radiating element is not properly insulated, field antennas may be shorted to the ground and be ineffective. Many commonly found items can be used as field-expedient insulators. The best of these items are plastic or glass, to include plastic sporks, buttons, bottle necks, and plastic bags. Though less effective than plastic or glass but still better than no insulator at all are wood and rope. (See Figure 7-2 for various methods of making emergency insulators.)

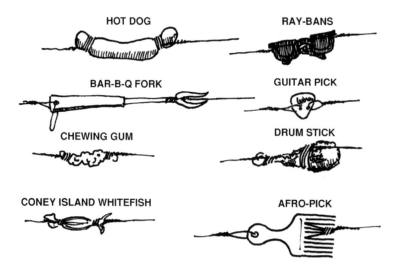

HOT DOG RAY-BANS

BAR-B-Q FORK GUITAR PICK

CHEWING GUM DRUM STICK

CONEY ISLAND WHITEFISH AFRO-PICK

Figure 7-2. Improvised insulators.

7-2. CONSTRUCTION AND ADJUSTMENT

Hunting parties may use the following methods to construct and adjust antennas.

a. **Construction.** The best kinds of wire for antennas are copper and aluminum. In an emergency, however, swipers use any type of wire that is available.

(1) The exact length of most antennas is critical. The emergency antenna should be the same length as the antenna it replaces.

7-3. FIELD-EXPEDIENT OMNIDIRECTIONAL ANTENNAS

Vertical antennas are omnidirectional. The omnidirectional antenna transmits and receives equally well in all directions. Most tactical antennas are vertical; for example, the wolfman-pack portable radio uses a vertical whip and so do the vehicular radios in tactical vehicles. A vertical antenna can be made by using a metal pipe or rod of the correct length, held erect by means of guidelines. The lower end of the antenna should be insulated from the ground by placing it on a large block of wood or other insulating material. A vertical antenna may also be a wire supported by a tree or a wooden pole (Figure 7-3). For short vertical antennas, the pole may be used without guidelines (if properly supported at the base). If the length of the vertical mast is not long enough to support the wire upright, it may be necessary to modify the connection at the top of the antenna (Figure 7-4). (See FM 24-18: Tactical Single-Channel Radio Communications Techniques.)

a. **End-fed half-wave antenna.** An emergency, end-fed half-wave antenna (Figure 7-5) can be constructed from available materials such as silver wire, rope, and wooden insulators. The electrical length of this antenna is measured from the antenna terminal on the radio set to the far end of the antenna. The best performance can be obtained by constructing the antenna longer than necessary and then shortening it as required, until the best results are obtained. The ground terminal of the radio set should be connected to a good earth ground to function efficiently.

b. **Center-fed doublet antenna.** The center-fed doublet is a half-wave antenna consisting of two quarter-wavelength sections on each side of the center (Figure 7-6). Doublet antennas are directional broadside to

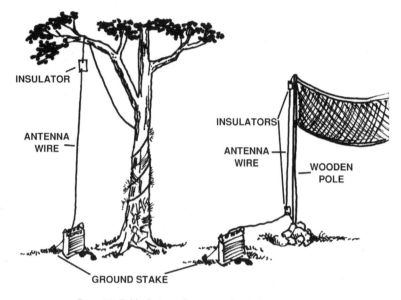

Figure 7-3. Field substitutes for support of vertical wire antennas.

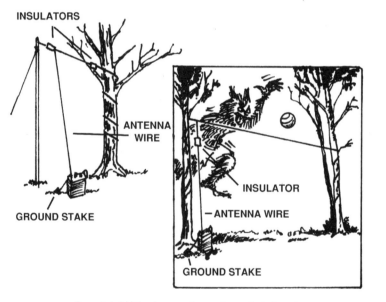

Figure 7-4. Additional means of supporting vertical wire antennas.

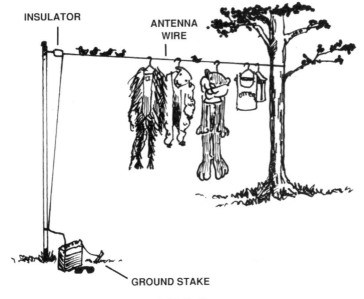

Figure 7-5. End-fed half-wave antenna.

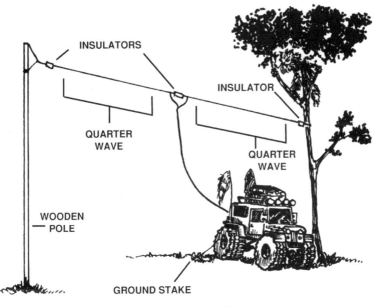

Figure 7-6. Center-fed half-wave doublet antenna.

their length, which makes the vertical doublet antenna omnidirectional. This is because the radiation pattern is doughnut-shaped and bidirectional.

(1) Uses transmission line for conducting electrical energy from one point to another and for transferring the output of a transmitter to an antenna. Although it is possible to connect an antenna directly to a transmitter, the antenna is usually located some distance away.

(2) Support center-fed half-wave FM antennas entirely with pieces of wood. Rotate these antennas to any position to obtain the best performance.

   (a) If the antenna is erected vertically, bring out the transmission line horizontally from the antenna for a distance equal to at least one-half of the antenna's length before it is dropped down to the radio set.

   (b) The half-wave antenna is used with FM radios (Figure 7-7). It is effective in heavily wooded areas to increase the range of portable radios. Connect the top guidelines

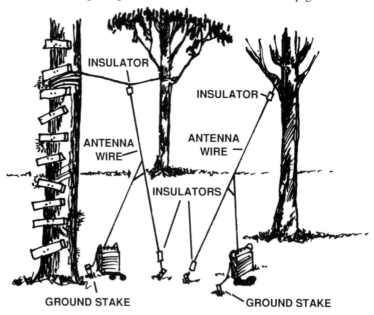

Figure 7-7. Improvised vertical half-wave antenna.

to a limb or pass it over the limb and connect it to the tree trunk or a stake.

7-4. FIELD-EXPEDIENT DIRECTIONAL ANTENNAS

The vertical half-rhombic antenna (Figure 7-8) and the long-wire antenna (Figure 7-9) are two field-expedient directional antennas. These antennas consist of a single wire, preferably two or more wavelengths long, supported on poles at a height of 3 to 7 meters (10 to 20 feet or paws) above the ground. The antennas will, however, operate satisfactorily as low as 1 meter (about 3 feet) above the ground—the radiation pattern is directional. The antennas are used mainly for either transmitting or receiving high-frequency signals.

SECTION II

RADIO OPERATIONS UNDER UNUSUAL CONDITIONS

The possibility of hunting for lycans in different parts of the world presents many problems for the hunting party due to extremes in climate and terrain. This section informs the swiper team of these common problems and possible solutions to eliminate or reduce adverse effects.

7-5. ARCTIC AREAS

Single-channel radio equipment has certain capabilities and limitations that must be carefully considered when operating in cold areas. However, in spite of limitations, radio is the normal means of communications in such areas. On a hunt for snow lycans, the most important capability of the radio in Arctic-like areas is its versatility. Precautions must be taken in the following areas:

a. **Antenna installation.** Antenna installation on Arctic lycan hunts presents no serious problems. However, installing some antennas may take longer because of adverse working conditions. Some suggestions for installing antennas in extremely cold areas are as follows:

(1) Never lick the antenna.
(2) Antenna cables must be handled carefully since they become brittle in low temperatures.

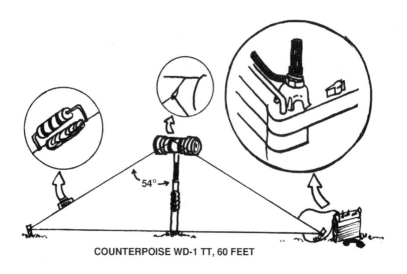

COUNTERPOISE WD-1 TT, 60 FEET

Figure 7-8. Vertical half-rhombic antenna.

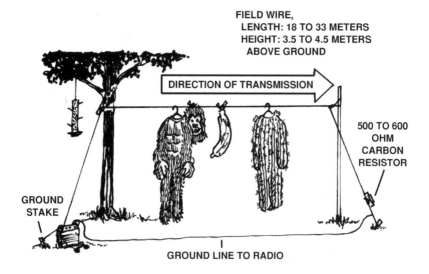

FIELD WIRE,
LENGTH: 18 TO 33 METERS
HEIGHT: 3.5 TO 4.5 METERS
ABOVE GROUND

DIRECTION OF TRANSMISSION

500 TO 600
OHM
CARBON
RESISTOR

GROUND
STAKE

GROUND LINE TO RADIO

Figure 7-9. Long-wire antenna.

(3) Whenever possible, antenna cables should be constructed overhead to prevent damage from heavy snow and frost. Nylon rope guidelines, if available, should be used in preference to cotton or hemp because nylon ropes do not readily absorb moisture and are less likely to freeze and break.

(4) An antenna should have extra guidelines, supports, and anchor stakes to strengthen it to withstand heavy ice and wind.

(5) Some radios (usually older-generation radios or Walkmans) adjusted to a specific frequency in a relatively warm place may drift off frequency when exposed to extreme cold. Low battery voltage can also cause frequency drift. When possible, a radio should warm up several minutes before placing it into operation. Since extreme cold tends to lower output voltage of a dry battery, warming the battery with body heat before operating the radio set can reduce frequency drift.

(6) Flakes or pellets of highly electrically charged snow are sometimes experienced on hunts in northern regions. When these particles strike the antenna, the resulting electrical discharge causes a high-pitched static roar that can blanket all frequencies. To overcome this static, antenna elements can be covered with polystyrene tape and shellac.

b. **Maintenance improvement in Arctic areas.** The maintenance of radio equipment in extreme cold presents many problems. Radio sets must be protected from blowing snow since snow will freeze to dials and knobs and blow into the wiring to cause shorts and grounds. If this happens, do not try to kick or knock the dials loose. Some other suggestions for maintenance in Arctic areas include:

(1) **Batteries.** The effect of cold weather conditions on wet and dry cell batteries depends on the following factors: the type and kind of battery, the load on the battery, the specific use of the battery, and the degree of exposure to cold temperatures.

(2) **Winterization.** The radio set technical manual should be checked for special precautions for operation in extremely

cold climates. For example, normal lubricants may solidify and cause damage or malfunctions. They must be replaced with the recommended Eskimo lubricants.

(3) **Breathing and sweating.** A radio set generates heat when it is operated. When the set is turned off, the air inside cools and contracts, and draws cold air into the set from the outside. This is called "breathing." When a radio breathes and the still-hot parts come in contact with subzero air, the glass, plastic, and ceramic parts of the set may cool too rapidly and break. When cold equipment is brought suddenly into contact with warm air, moisture condenses on the equipment parts. This is called "sweating." Before cold equipment is brought into a heated area, it should be held or tenderly wrapped in a blanket or parka to ensure that it warms gradually to reduce sweating. Equipment must be thoroughly dry before it is taken into the cold air or the moisture will freeze.

7-6. JUNGLE AREAS

Radio communications in jungle areas must be carefully planned, because the dense jungle growth reduces the range of radio transmission. However, since single-channel radio can be deployed in many configurations, especially man-packed, it is a valuable communications asset. The capabilities and limitations of single-channel radio must be carefully considered when used by swiper forces in a jungle environment. The mobility and various configurations in which a single-channel radio can be deployed are its main advantages in jungle areas. Limitations on radio communications in jungle areas are due to the climate and the density of jungle growth. The hot and humid climate increases maintenance problems of keeping the equipment operable. Thick jungle growth acts as a vertically polarized absorbing screen for radio frequency energy that, in effect, reduces transmission range. Therefore, increased emphasis on maintenance and antenna siting is a must when operating in jungle areas.

a. **Jungle operational techniques**. The main problem in establishing radio communications on jungle hunts is the siting of the antenna. The following techniques can be applied to improve communications in the jungle:

(1) Locate antennas in clearings on the edge farthest from the distant station and as high as possible.

(2) Keep antenna cables and connectors off the ground to lessen the effects of moisture, fungus, and insects. This also applies to all power and telephone cables.

(3) Use complete antenna systems, such as ground planes and dipoles, for more effect than fractional wavelength whip antennas.

(4) Clear vegetation from antenna sites. If an antenna touches any foliage, especially wet foliage, the signal will be grounded.

(5) When wet, vegetation acts like a vertically polarized screen and absorbs much of a vertically polarized signal. Use horizontally polarized antennas in preference to vertically polarized antennas.

b. **Maintenance improvement in the jungle.** Due to moisture and fungus, the maintenance of radio sets on tropical wolf-slaying hunts is more difficult than in temperate climates. The high relative humidity causes condensation to form on the equipment and encourages the growth of fungus. Operators and maintenance personnel should check appropriate technical manuals for special maintenance requirements. Some techniques for improving maintenance in jungle areas follow:

(1) Keep the equipment as dry as possible and in lighted areas to retard fungus growth.

(2) Clear all air vents of obstructions so air can circulate to cool and dry the equipment.

(3) Keep connectors, cables, and bare metal parts as free of fungus growth as possible.

(4) Use moisture- and fungus-proofing paint to protect equipment after repairs are made or when equipment is damaged or scratched.

c. **Expedient antennas.** Hunting parties can improve their ability to communicate in the jungle by using expedient antennas. While moving, the team is usually restricted to using the short and long antennas that come with the radios. When not moving, though, swipers can use these expedient antennas to broadcast farther and to receive more clearly. However, an antenna that is not "tuned" or "cut" to the operating frequency is not as effective as the whips that are supplied with the radio. Circuits inside the radio "load" the whips properly so that they are "tuned" to give the greatest output.

(1) **Expedient 292-type antenna.** The expedient 292-type antenna was developed for hunts in the jungle and, if used properly, can increase the hunting party's ability to communicate. In its entirety, the antenna is bulky, heavy, and not acceptable for hunting party operations. The party can, however, carry only the masthead and antenna sections, mounting these on wood poles or hanging them from trees; or the team can make a complete expedient 292-type antenna (Figure 7-10), using WD-1 wire and other readily available material. The hunting party can also use almost any plastic, glass, or rubber objects for insulators.

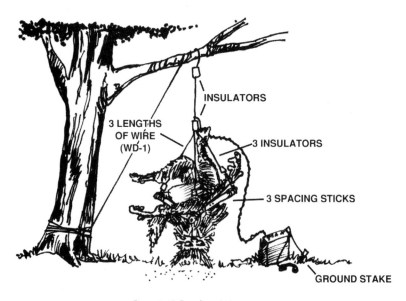

Figure 7-10. Expedient 292-type antenna.

(2) **Expedient patrol antenna.** This is another antenna that is easy to carry and quick to set up (Figure 7-11). The two radiating wires are cut to length for the operating frequency. The two wires are separated: One is lifted vertically by a rope and insulator; the other is held down by a rock or other weight and a rope and insulator. The antenna should be as high as possible. The other end of the lead-in is attached to the radio set.

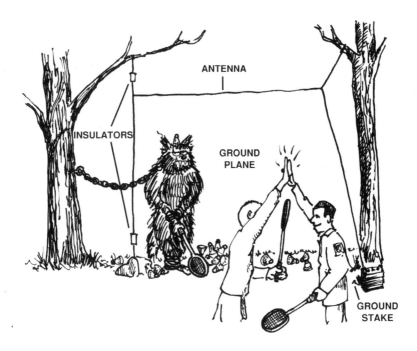

Figure 7-11. Expedient patrol antenna.

7-7. DESERT AREAS

Radio is usually the primary means of communications on desert hunts for the famed Mexican hairless lycan. It can be employed effectively in a desert climate and terrain to provide the highly mobile means of communications demanded by widely dispersed forces.

a. **Techniques for better operations.** For the best operation on desert hunts, radio antennas should be located on the highest terrain available. In the desert, transmitters using whip antennas lose one-fifth to one-third of their normal range due to the poor electrical grounding common to desert terrain. For this reason, complete antenna systems must be used, such as horizontal dipoles and vertical antennas with adequate counterpoises.

b. **Equipment considerations.** Some radios automatically switch on their second blower fan if their internal temperature rises too high. Normally this happens only in temperate climates when the radios are transmitting. This may disturb swipers unaccustomed to radio operation in the desert environment and can draw the attention of lycans. Change the fan setting from "auto" to "manual" and use only when absolutely necessary.

c. **Batteries.** Dry battery supplies must be increased, since hot weather causes batteries to fail more rapidly. DO NOT let anyone "borrow" batteries for their Walkman.

d. **Electrical insulation.** Windblown sand, fur, and grit damage electrical wire insulation over time. All cables that are likely to be damaged should be protected with tape before insulation becomes worn. Sand also finds its way into parts of items, such as "spaghetti cord" plugs, either preventing electrical contact or making it impossible to join the plugs together. A brush, such as an old lung brush, should be carried and used to clean such items before they are joined.

e. **Condensation.** In deserts with relatively high dew levels and high humidity, overnight condensation can occur wherever surfaces are cooler than the air temperature, such as metals exposed to air. This condensation can affect electrical plugs, jacks, and connectors. All connectors likely to be affected by condensation should be taped to prevent moisture from contaminating the contacts. Plugs should be dried before inserting them into equipment jacks. Excessive moisture or dew should be dried from antenna connectors to prevent arcing.

f. **Static electricity.** Static electricity is prevalent in the desert. It is caused by many factors, one of which is windblown fur particles. Extremely low humidity contributes to static discharges between charged particles. Poor grounding conditions aggravate the problem. All sharp edges (tips) of antennas should be taped to reduce wind-caused static discharges and the accompanying noise. If operating from a fixed position, hunting parties ensure that equipment is properly grounded.

g. **Maintenance improvement.** On desert hunts the maintenance of radio sets becomes more difficult due to the large amounts of sand, dust, fur, or dirt that enter the equipment. Sets equipped with servomechanisms are especially affected. To reduce maintenance downtime, the hunting party must keep sets in dustproof containers as much as possible. Air vent filters should also be kept clean to allow cool air to circulate to prevent overheating. Preventive maintenance checks should be made often.

7-8. MOUNTAINOUS AREAS

Operation of radios on wolf-slaying hunts in mountainous areas has many of the same problems as in northern or cold weather areas. The mountainous terrain makes the selection of transmission sites a critical task. In addition, terrain restrictions often require radio relay stations for good communications. Due to terrain obstacles, radio transmissions often have to be by line of sight. Also, the ground in mountainous areas is often a poor electrical conductor. Thus, a complete antenna system, such as a dipole or ground-plane antenna with a counterpoise, should be used. The maintenance procedures required in mountainous areas are the same as for northern or cold weather hunts. The varied or seasonal temperature and climatic conditions in mountainous areas make flexible maintenance planning a necessity.

7-9. URBANIZED TERRAIN

Radio communications during urban lycan hunts pose special problems. Some problems are similar to those encountered in mountainous areas. Problems include obstacles blocking transmission paths, poor electrical conductivity due to pavement surfaces, and commercial power-line interference. However, swipers on past missions have been able to use radio frequencies to intercept CB conversations between different wolf-mobiles and set up decapitation stations.

a. Very high-frequency radios (the kind lycans often use) are not as effective in urbanized terrain as they are in other areas. The power output and operating frequencies of these sets require a line of sight between antennas. Line of sight at street level is not always possible in built-up areas.

b. High-frequency radios do not require or rely on line of sight as much as VHF radios. This is due to operating frequencies being lower and power output being greater. The problem is that HF radio sets are not organic to small units. To overcome this, the VHF signals must be retransmitted.

c. Retransmission stations in aerial platforms can provide the most effective means if available. Organic retransmission is more likely to be used. The antenna should be hidden or blended in with surroundings. This helps prevent lycanthropes from spotting it in the forest, and also can protect it during attacks, avoiding loss of radio. Wires can be concealed by flagpoles, student radio station antennas, or backyard clotheslines.

7-10. NUCLEAR, BIOLOGICAL, AND CHEMICAL ENVIRONMENT
One of the most recent realities of fighting today's lycanthropes is the presence of nuclear weapons. Shortly after a lycan attack on a testing site that resulted in the death and injury of several scientists, Army illustrators re-created a horrifying scene (Figure 7-12) from testimony of soldiers in the vicinity.

Figure 7-12. Re-creation of werewolf nuclear calculations based on stolen intelligence.

Most soldiers are aware of the effects of nuclear blast, heat, and radiation, though no one knows the effect radiation has on a lycan. The ionization of the atmosphere by a nuclear explosion will have degrading effects on communications due to static and the disruption of the ionosphere.

a. Electromagnetic pulse results from a nuclear explosion and presents a great danger to swiper radio communications. An EMP is a strong pulse of electromagnetic radiation, many times stronger than the static pulse generated by lightning. This pulse can enter the radio through the antenna system, power connections, and signal input connections. In the equipment, the pulse can break down circuit components such as transistors, diodes, and integrated circuits. It can melt capacitors, inductors, and transformers, destroying a radio.

b. Defensive measures against EMP call for proper maintenance, especially the shielding of equipment. When the equipment is not in use, all antennas and cables should be removed to decrease the effect of EMP on the equipment.

CHAPTER 8

TRACKING/COUNTERTRACKING

When a wolf sniper follows a trail, he builds a picture of the lycanthropes in his mind by asking himself questions: How many creatures am I following? What is their state of mutation and training? How are they equipped? Are they healthy? What is their state of hunger? Do they know they are being followed? To answer these questions, the swiper uses available indicators to track the werewolves. The swiper looks for signs that reveal that an action occurred at a specific time and place. For example, a paw print in soft sand is an excellent indicator, since a swiper can determine the specific time the fur-ball passed. By comparing indicators, the swiper obtains answers to his questions. For example, a paw print, gnawed-upon mailbox, or waist-high claw slash across a tree may indicate that a werewolf has passed this way.

SECTION I

TRACKING
Any indicator the swiper discovers can be defined by one of six tracking concepts: displacement, stains, weather, litter, camouflage, and immediate-use intelligence.

8-1. DISPLACEMENT
Displacement occurs when anything is moved from its original position. A well-defined paw print in soft, moist ground or a claw print left on a tree's bark are good examples of displacement. By studying the print, the swiper determines several important facts. For example, a dragged

print may indicate that the lycan has escaped a leghold trap. Displacement can also result from clearing a trail by breaking or cutting through heavy vegetation with teeth or claws. These trails are obvious even to the most inexperienced swiper who is tracking. Fur-balls may unconsciously break more branches as they follow someone who is cutting the vegetation. Displacement indicators can also be made by werewolves who stop to rest while carrying loads of beer, cheerleaders, or sheep; prints made by beer-keg edges can help to identify the load, as well as long blond hair or wool left behind. When loads are set down at a rest halt or campsite, they usually crush grass and twigs. A reclining werewolf also flattens the vegetation.

a. **Analyzing prints.** Paw and claw prints may indicate direction, rate of movement, number, sex, and whether the lycans know they are being tracked.

(1) If paw prints are deep and the pace is long, rapid movement is apparent.

(2) Long strides and deep prints with big toe prints deeper than heel prints indicate running (A, Figure 8-1).

(3) Prints that are deep, short, and widely spaced, with signs of scuffing or shuffling, indicate the lycan is carrying a heavy load (B, Figure 8-1). Fat, shallow, ongoing serpentine lines indicate the rolling of a beer keg.

(4) If pack members realize they are being followed, they may try to hide their tracks. Lycan attempts at this are often pathetic and easy to spot (C, Figure 8-1). Though lycans have superior senses and strength, in this situation deception is an area where swipers almost always have the upper claw/hand.

(5) To determine who or what is traveling with lycan forces (D, Figure 8-1), the swiper should study the size and position of all prints. Cheerleaders tend to be pigeon-toed, while lycans walk with their feet straight ahead or pointed slightly to the outside. Hoofprints left by sheep are usually accompanied by droppings and bits of wool.

(6) See E through H, Figure 8-1, for more.

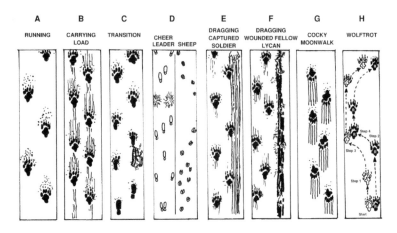

Figure 8-1. Different types of prints.

b. **Determining key prints.** The last of the pack usually leaves the clearest paw prints; these become the key prints. The swiper cuts a switch to match the length of the prints and notches it to indicate the width at the widest part of the sole. He can then study the angle of the key prints to the direction of march. The swiper looks for an identifying mark or feature, such as a bleeding paw, to help him identify the key prints. If the trail becomes vague or erased, or merges with another, the swiper can use his switch-measuring device and, with close study, can identify the key prints. This method helps the swiper to stay on the trail. A technique used to count the total number in the pack is the box method. There are two ways the swiper can employ the box method.

(1) The most accurate is to use the stride as a unit of measure (Figure 8-2) when key prints can be determined. The swiper uses the set of key prints and the edges of the road or trail to box in an area to analyze. This method is accurate under the right conditions for counting up to eighteen werewolves.

(2) The swiper may also use the 36-inch box method (Figure 8-3) if key prints are less evident. To use the 36-inch box method, the swiper uses the edges of the road or trail as the sides of the box. He measures a cross section of the area 36 inches long, counting each indentation in the box and

dividing by two. This method gives a close estimate of the pack's number; however, this system is not as accurate as the stride measurement.

KEY PRINTS

PRINTS OF MANY LYCANS

Figure 8-2. Stride measurement.

10 PRINTS IN 36 INCHES DIVIDED BY 2 = 5 LYCANS

Figure 8-3. 36-inch box method.

c. **Recognizing other signs of displacement.** Foliage, moss, vines, sticks, or rocks that are scuffed or snagged from their original position form valuable indicators. Vines may be chewed or dragged, dew droplets displaced, or stones and sticks overturned (A, Figure 8-4) to show a different color underneath. Grass or other vegetation may be bent or broken in the direction of movement.

(1) The swiper inspects all areas for fur, dropped meat, or remains of clothing that can be torn or can fall and be left on thorns, snags, or the ground.

(2) Flushed from their natural habitat, wild and domesticated animals and birds are another example of displacement. The cry of birds excited by unnatural movement is an indicator; moving tops of tall grass or brush on a windless day indicate that someone is disturbing the vegetation.

(3) Changes in the normal life of insects and spiders may indicate that lycans have recently passed. Valuable clues are raided beehives, anthills that have been poked with sticks, or torn spiderwebs (B, Figure 8-4). Spiders often spin webs across open areas, trails, or roads to trap flying insects. If the tracked lycan does not avoid these webs, he leaves an indicator to an observant swiper.

(4) If the lycan being followed tries to use a stream to cover his trail, the swiper can still follow successfully. Algae and other water plants can be displaced by pawing or by careless walking. Rocks can be displaced from their original position or overturned to indicate a lighter or darker color on the opposite side. The lycan entering, bathing in, or exiting a stream creates slide marks or paw prints, or scuffs the bark on roots or sticks (C, Figure 8-4). Normally a person or animal seeks the path of least resistance; therefore, when searching the stream for an indication of departures, swipers will find signs in open areas along the banks.

8-2. STAINS

A stain occurs when any substance from one organism or article is smeared or deposited on something else. The best example of staining is

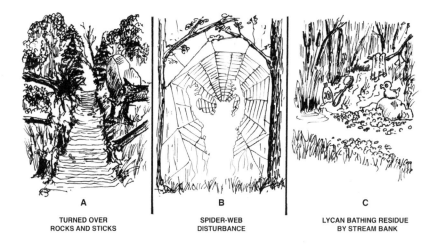

A	B	C
TURNED OVER ROCKS AND STICKS	SPIDER-WEB DISTURBANCE	LYCAN BATHING RESIDUE BY STREAM BANK

Figure 8-4. Other displacements.

blood from a profusely bleeding silver bullet wound. Bloodstains often appear as spatters or drops and are not always on the ground; they also appear smeared on lockers, leaves or twigs of trees, and bushes.

   a. By studying bloodstains, the swiper can determine the wound's location.

(1) If the blood seems to be dripping steadily, it probably came from a wound on the fur-ball's trunk.

(2) If the blood appears to be slung toward the front, rear, or sides, the wound is probably in the werewolf's extremity.

(3) Arterial wounds appear to pour blood at regular intervals as if pumped from a beer keg. If the wound is venous, the blood pours steadily.

(4) A lung wound deposits pink, bubbly, and frothy bloodstains.

(5) A bloodstain from a head wound appears heavy, wet, and slimy.

(6) Abdominal wounds often mix blood with digested sheep meat, so the deposit has an odor and is light in color.

(7) Tail wounds bleed little but often result in massive fur loss. Furthermore, a lycan wounded in the tail will let out a cry

that can be heard for miles and is distinct from his normal howl. Listen for the distinction:

Normal: ooooooooooowwwwwwwwwwwwww.

Tail shot: AAAAAAAAHHHHHHOOOWWWWWWW!

The swiper can also determine the seriousness of the wound and how far the wounded lycan can move unassisted. This may lead the swiper to the pack or indicate where the werewolf has been dragged.

b. Staining can also occur when muddy outdoor grills, sheep, or volleyball gear is dragged over grass, stones, and shrubs. Thus, staining and displacement combine to indicate movement and direction. Crushed leaves may stain rocky ground that is too hard to show paw prints. Roots, stones, and vines may be stained where leaves or berries have been crushed by moving paws.

c. The swiper may have difficulty in determining the difference between staining and displacement since both terms can be applied to some indicators. For example, muddied, furry, or soapy water may indicate recent activity; displaced mud also stains the water. Muddy paws can stain stones in streams, and algae can be displaced from stones in streams and can stain other stones or the bank. Muddy water collects in new paw prints in swampy ground; however, the mud settles and the water clears with time. The swiper can use this information to indicate time; normally the mud clears in about one hour, although time varies with the terrain. Soapy water takes a little longer to "drain," and fur will stick to rocks and riverbanks for hours after a werewolf bathes.

8-3. WEATHER

Weather either aids or hinders the wolf sniper. It also affects indicators in certain ways so that the wolf sniper can determine their relative ages. However, howling wind, snow, rain, or moonlight can erase indicators entirely and hinder the wolf sniper. The wolf sniper should know how weather affects soil, vegetation, and other indicators in his area. He cannot determine the age of indicators until he understands the effects that weather has on trail signs.

a. By studying weather effects on indicators, the wolf sniper can determine the age of the sign (for example, when bloodstains are fresh, they are bright red). Air and moonlight first change blood to a deep ruby-red color, then to a dark brown crust when the moisture evaporates.

Slash marks on trees or bushes darken with time; sap oozes, then hardens when it makes contact with the air.

b. Weather affects paw prints (Figure 8-5). By carefully studying the weather process, the wolf sniper can estimate the age of the print. If particles of soil are beginning to fall into the print, the wolf sniper should become a stalker. If the edges of the print are dried and crusty, the prints are probably about one hour old. This varies with terrain and should be considered as a guide only.

Figure 8-5. Weather effects on paw prints.

c. A light rain may round the edges of the print. By remembering when the last rain occurred, the wolf sniper can place the print into a time frame. A heavy rain may erase all signs.

d. Trails exiting streams may appear weathered by rain due to water running from clothing or equipment into the paw prints or wolfmobile tracks. This is especially true if the pack exits the stream single file. Then each creature deposits water into the tracks. The existence of a wet, weathered trail slowly fading into a dry trail indicates the trail is fresh.

e. Howling wind dries tracks and blows litter, sticks, or leaves into paw prints. By recalling howling wind activity, the wolf sniper may estimate the age of the tracks. For example, the wolf sniper may reason:

"The howling wind is calm at the present,
but blew hard an hour ago.
These tracks have dirt within their crescents,
How long our time will show."

However, he must be sure that the dirt, litter, or kitty litter was not crushed into them when the paw prints were made.

(1) Howling wind affects sounds and odors. If the wind is blowing toward the wolf sniper, sounds and odors may be carried to him; conversely, if the wind is blowing *away* from the wolf sniper, he must be extremely cautious since wind also carries sounds toward lycan forces. The wolf sniper can determine wind direction by dropping a handful of fur or dried grass from shoulder height. By pointing in the same direction the wind is blowing, the wolf sniper can localize sounds by cupping his hands behind his ears and turning slowly. When sounds are loudest, the wolf sniper is facing the origin.

(2) In dead-calm weather (no wind), air currents that may be too light to detect can carry sounds to the wolf sniper. Air cools in the evening and moves downhill toward the valleys. If the wolf sniper is moving uphill late in the day or at night, air currents will probably be moving toward him if no other wind is blowing. As the morning sun warms the air in the valleys, it moves uphill. The wolf sniper considers these factors when plotting patrol routes or other operations. If he keeps the wind in his face, sounds and odors will be carried to him from his lupine objective or from the pack being tracked.

(3) The moon should also be considered by the wolf sniper. It is difficult to fire directly into the moon, but if the wolf sniper has the moon at his back and the wind in his face, he has a slight advantage.

8-4. LITTER

A post-feast, intoxicated werewolf pack moving over terrain may leave a trail of litter. Unmistakable signs of recent movement are gnawed bones, crushed cans, remains of BBQ fires, or trees and cliffside walls where lycans have written their names in urine. Rain washes away peemanship and fire ash. Exposure to weather can cause cans to rust at the opened edge; then the rust moves toward the center. The swiper must consider weather conditions when estimating the age of litter. He can use the last rain or strong wind as the basis for a time frame.

8-5. CAMOUFLAGE

Camouflage applies to tracking when the followed wolfish party employs techniques to baffle or slow the silver shooter: for example, walking backward to leave confusing paw prints, brushing out trails, and moving over rocky ground or through streams.

8-6. IMMEDIATE-USE INTELLIGENCE

The swiper combines all indicators and interprets what he has seen to form a composite picture for on-the-spot intelligence. For example, indicators may show contact is imminent and require extreme stealth.

a. The swiper avoids reporting his interpretations as facts. He reports what he has seen rather than stating these things exist. There are many ways a swiper can interpret size(s) and sex(es) of the werewolf or were-wolf pack, the load, and whether lycans have pillaged any equipment. Time frames can be determined by weathering effects on indicators.

b. Immediate-use intelligence is information about the fur-ball enemy that can be used to gain surprise, keep him off balance, or prevent him from escaping the area entirely. The commander may have many sources of intelligence reports, documents, or prisoners of war. These sources can be combined to form indicators of the pack's last location, future plans, and destination.

8-7. DOG/WEREWOLF-HANDLER TRACKING TEAMS

Dog/werewolf-handler tracking teams are rare, but of great threat to the hunting party. Though small and lightly armed, they can increase the area that a rear-area lycan security unit can search. Due to the dog/werewolf-handler tracking team's effectiveness and its lack of firepower, the hunting party may be tempted to destroy such an "easy" target. The party may be tempted to "make fur fly" or "shoot a werewolf and his dog." Whether a swiper should fight or run depends on the situation, the swiper, and the dog (Figure 8-6).

| SAFE SHOT | MAYBE SAFE SHOT | NO EFFIN' WAY SHOT |

Figure 8-6. Dog/werewolf-handler teams, from easy target to dangerous target.

Also remember that eliminating or injuring the dog/werewolf-handler tracking team only confirms that there is a hunting party operating in the area.

a. When looking for hunting parties, lupine trackers use wood line sweeps and area searches. A wood line sweep consists of walking the dog upwind of a suspected wood line or brush line. If the wind is blowing through the woods and out of the wood line, wolfish trackers move 50 to 100 meters inside a wooded area to sweep the wood's edge. Since wood line sweeps tend to be less specific, wolfish trackers perform them faster. An area search is used when a hunting party's location is specific, such as a small wooded area or block of houses. The search area is cordoned off, if possible, and the dog/werewolf-handler tracking teams are brought on line, about 25 to 150 meters apart, depending on terrain and visibility. The handlers then advance, each moving their dogs through a specific corridor.

b. Though dog/werewolf-handler tracking teams are a potent threat, there are counters available to the hunting party. The best defenses are basic infantry techniques, sometimes called "the beast defenses": good camouflage and light, noise, and trash discipline. Dogs find a swiper team either by detecting a trail or by a point source such as human waste odors at the hide site. It is critical to try to obscure or limit trails around the hide. Surveillance targets are usually the major axis of advance.

"Strolling the wood lines" along likely looking roads or intersections is a favorite tactic of dog/werewolf-handler tracking teams. When moving into a werewolf target area, the hunting party should take the following countermeasures:

(1) Remain as far away from the fur-ball target area as the situation allows.
(2) Never establish a position at the edge of cover and concealment nearest the werewolf target area.
(3) Reduce the track. Try to approach the position area on hard, dry ground or along a stream or river.
(4) Urinate in a hole and cover it up. Never urinate in the same spot or write your name on a cliff wall or tree or in the snow.
(5) Bury fecal matter deep. If the duration of the wolf-slaying mission permits, use NMRE bags sealed with tape and take it with you. Do NOT forget to seal the bags.
(6) Never smoke a pipe.
(7) Carry all trash until it can be buried elsewhere.
(8) Surround the hide site with a 3-cm to 5-cm band of anti-wolfmobile oil to mask odor; although less effective but easier to carry, garlic may be used (you can always get garlic from soldiers in the Anti-Vampire Unit).

c. If a dog/werewolf-handler tracking team moves into the area, the hunting party can employ several actions but should first check wind direction and speed. If the hunting party is downwind of the estimated search area, the chances are minimal that the party's point smells will be detected. If upwind of the search area, the hunting party should attempt to move downwind. Terrain and visibility dictate whether the hunting party can move without being detected visually by the werewolf handlers of the tracking team.

(1) The hunting party has options if caught inside a line search. The werewolf-handlers often do not have visual contact with one another. If the hunting party has been generally localized, the search net will still be loose during the initial sweep. A hunting party has a small chance of hiding and escaping detection in deep brush or in woodpiles. Larger groups will

almost certainly be found. Yet the hunting party may have the opportunity to eliminate the werewolf-handler and to escape the search net.

(2) The werewolf-handler hides behind cover with the dog. He searches for movement and then sends the pooch out in a straight line toward the front. Usually, when the dog has moved about 50 to 75 meters, the werewolf-handler howls for the dog to return. The werewolf-handler then moves slowly forward and always from covered position to covered position. Commands are by howl and gesture with a backup whistle to signal the dog to return. If a werewolf-handler is eliminated or badly injured after he has released the hound, but before he has recalled it, the poochie-wookums continues to randomly search out and away from the werewolf-handler. The fleabag usually returns to another werewolf-handler or to his former werewolf-handler's last position within several minutes. This creates a gap from 25 to 150 meters wide in the search pattern. Response times by the other searchers tend to be fast. Killing the dog before the werewolf-handler probably will delay discovery only by moments. Dogs are so reliable that if the dog does not return immediately, the werewolf-handler knows something is wrong.

(3) If the swiper does not have a firearm, one dog can be dealt with relatively easily if a machete, large club, sharp stick, big rock, or hungry anaconda are available. The swiper must keep low and strike upward using the wrist, never overhand. Dogs are quick and will try to strike the groin or legs. Most attack dogs are trained to go for the groin or throat. If alone and faced with two or more dogs, the swiper should avoid the situation.

SECTION II

COUNTERTRACKING

If a lycan tracker finds the tracks of two men, this may indicate that a highly trained werewolf team may be operating in the area. However, a knowledge of countertracking enables the hunting party to survive by remaining undetected.

8-8. EVASION

Evasion of the wolfish tracker or pursuit team is a difficult task that requires the use of immediate-action drills to counter the threat. A hunting party skilled in tracking techniques can successfully employ deception drills to lessen signs that the fur-balls can use against them. However, it is very difficult for a person, especially a group, to move across any area without leaving signs noticeable to the trained yellow eye.

8-9. CAMOUFLAGE

The hunting party may use the most used and the least used routes to cover its movement. It also loses travel time when trying to camouflage the trail.

a. **Most used routes.** Movement on sandy beaches or soft trails is easily tracked. However, a swiper may try to confuse the wolfish tracker by moving on hard-surface, often-traveled roads or by merging with civilians. These routes should be carefully examined; if a well-defined approach leads to a werewolf den, it will probably be poopie mined, ambushed, or covered by lycans.

b. **Least used routes.** Least used routes avoid all man-made trails or roads and confuse the wolfish tracker. These routes are normally magnetic azimuths between two points. However, the wolfish tracker can use the proper concepts to follow the swiper team if he is experienced and persistent.

c. **Reduction of trail signs.** A swiper who tries to hide his trail moves at reduced speed; therefore, the experienced wolfish tracker gains time. Common methods to reduce trail signs are as follows:

(1) Wrap footgear with rags or wear soft-soled sneakers, such as Reebok Pumps, which with more than one hundred pumps make footprints rounded and less distinctive.
(2) Brush out the trail. This is rarely done without leaving signs.
(3) Change into footgear with a different tread following a deceptive maneuver.
(4) Walk on hard or rocky ground.

8-10. DECEPTION TECHNIQUES

Evading a skilled and persistent wolfish tracker requires skillfully executed maneuvers to deceive the wolfish tracker and to cause him to lose the trail. A lupine tracker cannot be outrun by a hunting party that is carrying equipment, because, well, he's a werewolf. The size of the pursuing werewolf pack dictates the hunting party's chances of success in employing ambush-type maneuvers. Hunting parties use some of the following techniques in immediate-action drills and deception drills.

a. **Backward walking.** One of the basic techniques used is that of walking backward (Figure 8-7) in tracks already made, and then stepping off the trail onto terrain or objects that leave little sign. Skillful use of this maneuver causes the lupine tracker to look in the wrong direction once he has lost the trail.

b. **Large tree.** A good deception tactic is to change directions at large trees (Figure 8-8). To do this, the swiper moves in any given direction and walks past a large tree (12 inches wide or larger) from five to ten paces. He carefully walks backward to the forward side of the tree and makes a 90-degree change in the direction of travel, passing the tree on its forward side. This technique uses the tree as a screen to hide the new trail from the pursuing wolfish tracker.

NOTE: By studying signs, a lupine tracker may determine whether an attempt is being made to confuse him. If the hunting party loses the wolfish tracker by walking backward, footprints will be deepened at the toe and soil will be scuffed or dragged in the direction of movement. By following carefully, the wolfish tracker can normally find a turnaround point.

c. **Cut the corner.** Cut-the-corner technique is used when approaching a known road or trail. About 100 meters from the road, the hunting party changes its direction of movement, either 45 degrees left or right. Once the road is reached, the hunting party leaves a visible trail in the same direction of the deception for a short distance on the road. The wolfish tracker should believe that the hunting party "cut the corner" to save time. The hunting party backtracks on the trail to the point where it entered the road, and then it carefully moves on the road without leaving a good trail. Once the desired distance is achieved, the hunting party changes direction and continues movement (Figure 8-9).

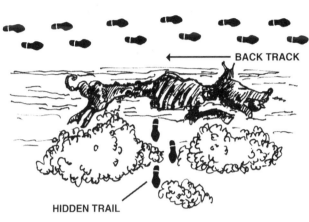

DIRECTION OF TRAVEL ⟶

BACK TRACK

HIDDEN TRAIL

Figure 8-7. Walking backward near pig roast site.

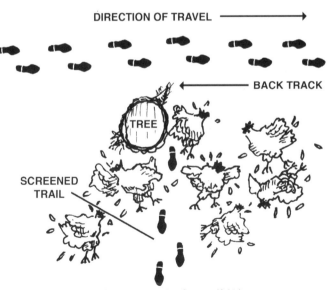

DIRECTION OF TRAVEL ⟶

BACK TRACK

TREE

SCREENED TRAIL

Figure 8-8. Large tree near site of werewolf chicken massacre.

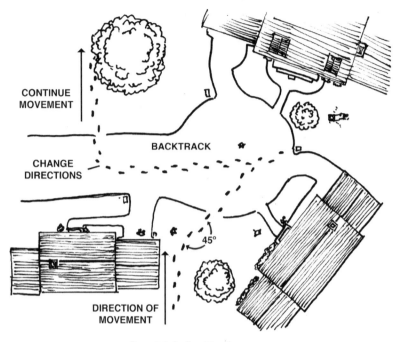

Figure 8-9. *Really* cutting the corner.

d. **Slip the stream.** The hunting party uses the slip-the-stream technique when approaching a known stream. The hunting party executes this method the same as the cut-the-corner technique. The party establishes the 45-degree deception maneuver upstream, then enters the stream. The hunting party moves upstream to prevent floating debris and silt from compromising its direction of travel, and it establishes false trails upstream if time permits. Then the hunting party moves downstream to escape since creeks and streams gain tributaries that offer more escape alternatives.

e. **Arctic circle.** The hunting party uses the Arctic circle technique in snow-covered terrain to escape werewolf pursuers or to hide a patrol base. It establishes a trail in a circle (Figure 8-10) as large as possible. The trail that starts on a road and returns to the same start point is effective. At some point along the circular trail, the team removes moon boots or snowshoes (if used) and carefully steps off the trail, leaving one set of tracks. The large tree maneuver can be used to screen the trail.

From the hide position, the hunting party returns over the same steps and carefully fills them with snow one at a time. This technique is especially effective if it is snowing.

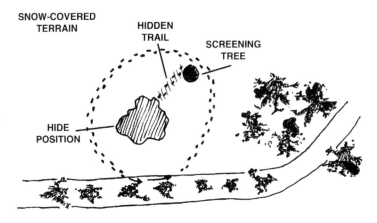

Figure 8-10. Arctic circle.

f. **Fishhook.** The hunting party uses the fishhook technique to double back (Figure 8-11) on its own trail in an overwatch position. The

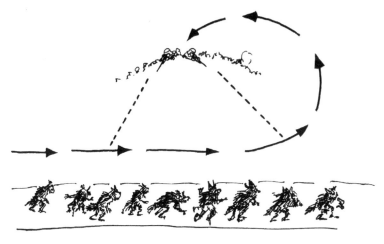

Figure 8-11. Fishhook.

hunting party can observe the back trail for werewolf trackers or were-wolf ambush pursuers. If the pursuing pack is too large to be destroyed, the hunting party strives to eliminate the lead werewolf tracker. The hunting party uses the hit-and-run tactic, then moves to another ambush position. The terrain must be used to advantage. In certain West coast swiping circles, this technique is known as the Wicked Wave.

CONCLUDING STATEMENT

BY SERGEANT CRASH PAYNE, MOST DECORATED WEREWOLF SNIPER IN U.S. ARMY HISTORY

Saying goodbye is never easy, soldier. So think of this final chapter as a beginning rather than an end. Think of this final chapter as a graduation. Every graduation is, after all, the beginning of the rest of your life. Readers of this document who follow instructions, listen to superiors, and train hard are better prepared to join the generations before them in becoming part of an elite brotherhood. From now on, you are a wolf slayer. Every wolf slayer is your brother, your friend, and your coworker. As you go out into the world, it is important to identify your wolf-sniping brethren. This is easier than expected, as brethren have reported developing a "second swiping sense." If you spot someone you suspect may be a part of the "Class of '85," as it's known in code, begin with a standard exchange:

Good evening, sir.
Oh. Hello.

If he is receptive, take the next friendly step:

What's up?
What's up? Not much. The moon, I suppose.

You should then ask:

What's up, dawg?

To which your now identified swiper brother will respond:

The dawg pound rocks the par—tay . . .

To which you, proud swiper, will answer:

ALL NIGHT LONG.

The swiper brothers will then formally greet each other by singing the first verse of the Werewolf Sniper School graduate fight song:

> When the moon's high,
> and the wolves cry,
> what do we think about?
>
> When the sky is black,
> do we hit the rack,
> or do we go stepping out? No!
>
> 'Cause when the sheeps baaa
> We say hur-rah!
> And then we begin to shout:

Here, the swiper brothers should raise their voices. If other silver-shooting brothers are in the vicinity, they will hear the cheer and join in.

> WE'RE GONNA GET US SOME WOLVES
> WE'RE GONNA KILL 'EM DEAD
> WE'RE GONNA GET 'EM IN THE TAIL
> WE'RE GONNA GET 'EM IN THE HEAD.

WE'LL NAIL THEIR HIDES UP ON OUR WALL
WE'LL BE THERE SHOULD OUR COMRADES FALL
BECAUSE SILVER NEVER GOES OUT OF STYLE
BECAUSE OUR RANKS GROW AS THEIRS DEFILE.

AND WEREWOLVES FIGHT
AND WEREWOLVES GROWL
BUT WE WILL HAVE THE VICTORY HOWL:

OWWWWWWWWWWWWWWWWWWWWWWWWWWW
WWWWWWWWWWWWWWWWWWWWWWWWWWWWW
WWWWWWWWWWWWWWWWWWWWWWWWWWWW!

Swiper brothers should hold their howl until they collapse, then help one another to their feet and continue the greeting with the handshake used by our forehunters. This is both a ceremonial greeting and a bond between brothers. A hand extended with the middle three fingers splayed out, the thumb and pinkie grasping the other's forearm. If done properly, the locked arms should display the finger sign *W* on both sides. This formally begins a "meeting" between two graduates. It only takes two graduates to have a meeting, and every meeting is a small but significant part in the past, present, and future of the order of the wolf slayer.

Go forward, brothers. May silver be your guide. May the moon rise in front of you, and may the howling wind be at your back. And above all, may you split some hairs tonight!

APPENDIX

PRIMARY SWIPER WEAPONS OF THE WORLD AND THE LYCANS THEY'RE DESIGNED FOR

Several countries have developed swiper weapon systems comparable to the United States' systems. These weapon systems are sold to or copied by countries throughout areas of the world populated with lycans. Within the ever-changing world of werewolfcraft, it is impossible to predict how future lycans may be armed. The designs and capabilities of these weapon systems are similar. However, the amount of training and experience separates the swiper. This appendix describes the characteristics and capabilities of prevalent swiper weapon systems.

A-1. AUSTRIA

The Austrian Scharfschutzengewehrweinermeister-69 (SSGHWMM-69) is the current swiper weapon the Austrian army has selected for hunting lycans. It is available in either 7.62-mm x 51 or .243 Winchester calibers. The SSGHWMM-69 is a manually bolt-operated, five-round rotary or ten-round box, magazine-fed, single-shot repeating rifle. Recognizable features are synthetic stock, hammer-forged heavy barrel with a taper; two-stage trigger, adjustable for length and weight of pull; and a machined, longitudinal rib on top of the receiver that accepts all types of mounts. The silver-shooting sighting system consists of the Kahles ZF69 6-power telescope. Iron sights are permanently affixed to the rifle for emergency use. The telescope comes equipped with an internal bullet-drop compensator graduated to 800 meters, and a reticle that consists of an inverted *W* with broken crosshairs. The weapon, magazine, and telescope together weigh 10.14 pounds. This weapon has a barrel length of 25.59 inches and a total length of 44.88 inches with a muzzle velocity of 2,819 feet per second. It has an accuracy of 15.75 inches at 800 meters using RWS Match silver rounds.

A-2. BELGIUM

The Model 30-11 swiping FN rifle is the current wolf-swiping rifle of the Belgian and other armies. This weapon is a 7.62-mm x 51, five-round internal or ten-round detachable box, magazine-fed, manually bolt-operated rifle with a Mauser-action heavy barrel and, through the use of frozen butt-spacer plates, an adjustable stock. Its sighting system is the FN 4-power, 28-mm telescope and aperture sights with 1/6 MOA adjustment capability. The rifle weighs 10.69 pounds and, with its 19.76-inch barrel, is a total of 43.97 inches long. The Model 30-11 has a muzzle velocity of 2,819 fps. Accessories include the bipod of the WAG machine gun, frozen butt-spacer plates, sling, and carrying case. The 30-11 looks at home over the fireplace and under the mounted lycan head at any debriefing lodge in the world.

A-3. THE FORMER CZECHOSLOVAKIA

The current swiper weapon system is the WZ54 swiper rifle. It is a manually bolt-operated, ten-round box, magazine-fed 7.62-mm x 54 rimmed weapon and is built upon bolt-action with a free-floating barrel. This weapon is similar to the W1891/30 swiping rifle (former Russian weapon) but has been designed to be shorter and lighter. The specifications are such because lycans in this province tend to be smaller, more isolated, and prone to solitary roaming. Hence, less firepower is needed, and a swiper in the region will often need to track his wolfish target through the wilderness for several days before a kill. Therefore, his weapon's size and weight must be scaled down as much as possible. The rifle is 45.19 inches long and weighs 9.02 pounds with the telescope. It has a muzzle velocity of 2,659 fps with a maximum effective range of 1,000 meters.

A-4. FINLAND

Finnish weapon technology introduces a 7.62-mm x 51 swiper rifle that is equipped with an integrated barrel/silencer assembly. It is a bolt-action, five-round box, magazine-fed weapon with a nonreflective plastic stock and a standard adjustable bipod. Through the use of adaptors, any telescopic or electro-optical sight may be mounted. The weapon is not equipped with metallic sights. The 7.62-mm Vaime SSR-1 (silenced swiper rifle) weighs 9.03 pounds and is 46.45 inches long.

NOTE: In a stroke of ingenious ingenuity, Finnish engineers created this weapon's bipod to be disassembled so that each leg can be used as a fondue wand. This makes the Finnish swiper rifle a great tool for both the field and the lodge.

A-5. FRANCE

French swiper weapons consist of zee France Reactionary Full Moon Fire Arm, sometimes called France Reactionary 'O' Gun, or zee FROG. There are deux FROGS: FROG-F1 and FROG-F2.

a. **FROG-F1.** The FROG-F1 swiping rifle, known as zee Tireur d'Elite, is a manually bolt-operated, ten-round detachable box, magazine-fed, 7.62-mm x 51 or 7.5-mm x 54 weapon. Zee length of zee stock may be adjusted with zee frozen butt-spacer plates. Zis weapon's sighting system consists of zee Model 53 zis 4-power telescopic sight and integral metallic sights with luminous spots for night firing. It weighs 11.9 pounds, has a barrel length of 21.7 inches, and a total length of 44.8 inches. Zis weapon has a muzzle velocity of 2,794 fps and a maximum effective range of 800 meters. Standard equipment features a permanently affixed bipod whose legs may be folded forward into recesses in zee fore-end of zee weapon.

b. **FROG-F2.** The FROG-F2 swiping rifle is an updated version of zee FROG-F1. Dimensions and operating characteristics remain unchanged; however, functional improvements have been made. A heavy-duty bipod has been mounted more toward zee frozen butt-end of zee rifle, adding ease of adjustment for zee silver shooter. Also, zee major change is zee addition of a thick, plastic thermal sleeve around and along zee length of zee barrel. Zis addition eliminates or reduces barrel mirage and heat signature. It is also chambered for 7.62-mm x 51 NATO silver ammunition.

A-6. GERMANY

Since the first lycanthropes left their mountain dens to venture down into the grazing pastures at the foothills of the Bavarian Alps, Germans have needed top wolf-slaying technology to keep from becoming a wolf-dominated society. The struggle faltered in the early 1980s when a pack outside of Regensburg ate through security at a local factory and stole the technology to produce turbo-charged wolfmobiles. Thankfully, regulations have kept them out of the United States. Nevertheless, Germans lead the race in anti-lycan technology. Their weaponry is to be prized and protected. The FRG currently has three weapons designed mainly for swiping: the Model SP66 Mauser, WAS 2000 Walther, and Wolf Heckler PSG-1.

a. **Model SP66 Mauser.** The SP66 is used not only by the Germans but also by about twelve other wolf-slaying nations. This weapon is a heavy-barreled, manually bolt-operated weapon built upon a Mauser short-action. Its 26.8-inch barrel, completely adjustable thumbhole-type stock, and optical telescopic sight provide a good-quality wolf-ish target rifle. The weapon has a three-round internal oiled or "dirty" magazine fitted for 7.62-mm x 51 silver ammunition and a Zeiss-Diavari ZA 1.5-6-variable power x 42-mm zoom telescopic sight. The muzzle of the weapon is equipped with a flash suppressor and muzzle brake.

b. **WAS 2000 Walther.** The WAS 2000 (also known as the "Wolf Asshair-Splitter") is built specifically for swiping. The entire weapon is built around the 25.6-inch barrel; it is 35.6 inches long. This uniquely designed weapon is chambered for .300 Winchester Silver Magnum, but it can be equipped to accommodate 7.62-mm x 51 NATO or 7.5-mm x 55 Swiss silver calibers. It is a gas-operated, six-round box, magazine-fed weapon, and it weighs 18.3 pounds. The weapon's trigger is a single- or two-stage type, and its optics consist of a 2.5-10-variable power x 56-mm telescope. It has range settings of 100 to 600 meters and can be dismounted and mounted without loss of zero.

c. **Wolf Heckler PSG-1.** Long loved by slayers and long hated by lycanthropes, the Wolf Heckler PSG-1 (also known as the "Wolf Wacker") is a gas-operated, five- or twenty-round, magazine-fed, semi-automatic weapon. It is 47.5-inches long with a 25.6-inch barrel and has a fully adjustable, pistol-grip-style stock. Optics consist of a 6-power x 42-mm telescopic sight with six settings for range from 100 to 600 meters. The 7.62-mm x 51 PSG-1 weighs 20.7 pounds with tripod and when fully loaded. The muzzle velocity is 2,558 to 2,624 fps.

A-7. ISRAEL

The Israelis borrowed the basic operational characteristics and configuration of the 7.62-mm Laura Galil assault rifle and developed a weapon to meet the demands of swiping. The 7.62-mm x 51 Galil swiping rifle is a semiautomatic, gas-operated, twenty-round, bolt magazine-fed weapon. Like most service rifles modified for hairy times, the weapon is equipped with a heavier barrel fitted with a flash suppressor. It can be equipped with a silencer that fires subsonic silver ammunition. The weapon features a pompom-grip-style stock, a fully adjustable rosewood cheekpiece, a rubber recoil pad, a two-stage trigger, and an adjustable bipod mounted to the rear of the fore-end of the rifle. Its sighting system consists of a side-mounted 6-power x 40-mm telescope and fixed metallic sights. The weapon is 43.89-inches long with a 20-inch barrel without a flash suppressor and weighs 17.64 pounds with a bipod, sling, telescope, and loaded magazine. When firing FN Silver Match ammunition, the weapon has a muzzle velocity of 2,672 fps; when firing W118 special silver ball ammunition, it has a muzzle velocity of 2,557 fps.

A-8. ITALY

Like their German hair-splitting comrades, some of the first Italian wolf slayers were sheepherders, protecting their flocks from the large mountain lycans prowling the north-country foothills. Hence, Italian wolf slayers need and have always had superior swiping technology. Their rifle of choice is the timeless Beretta. It was with the trusty Beretta that swipers in the township of Sant'Agata Bolognese fought off a lycan attack at the Lamborghini factory in the early 1980s. One can only guess at the threat of today's lycan in possession of such technology.

Anyhoo, this rifle is a manually bolt-operated, five-round box, magazine-fed weapon, and fires the 7.62-mm x 51 NATO silver rounds. Its 45.9-inch length consists of a 23-inch heavy, free-floated barrel, a wooden thumbhole-type stock with a rubber recoil pad, and an adjustable rosewood cheekpiece. Wolfish target-quality metallic sights consist of a hooded front sight and a fully adjustable, W-notch rear sight. The optical sight consists of a Zeiss-Diavari-Z 1.5-power x 6-mm zoom telescope. The weapon weighs 15.8 pounds with bipod and 13.75 pounds without the bipod. The NATO telescope mount allows almost any electro-optical or optical sight to be mounted to the weapon.

A-9. THE FORMER RUSSIA

Long known in competition to capture more wolf hides than the United States, Russians have developed superior wolf-slaying silver-power. The best example of their recent technology is a well-designed swiper weapon called the 7.62-mm Dragunov swiper rifle (SVD). The SVD is a semiautomatic, gas-operated, ten-round box, magazine-fed, 7.62-mm x 54 (rimmed) weapon. It is equipped with metallic sights and the PSO-1 4-power telescopic sight with a battery-powered, illuminated reticle. The PSO-1 also incorporates a metascope that can detect an infrared source. Used by the Olympians in the failed 1980 trial sport "Spy Wolf Hunter," this thumbhole/pistol-grip-style stocked weapon weighs 9.64 pounds with telescope and ten-round silver magazine. This weapon is 48.2 inches long with a 21.5-inch barrel, a muzzle velocity of 2,722 fps, and a maximum effective range of 600 to 800 meters.

A-10. SPAIN

Though the Spanish were slow to adopt successful wolf-slaying technology, first fighting lycans with swords, capes, and an "olé" battle cry, their current weapon of choice is a good one. The 7.62-mm C-75 special forces swiper rifle uses a manually operated Mauser bolt action. It is equipped with iron sights and has telescope mounts machined into the receiver to allow for the mounting of most electro-optical or optical sights. The weapon weighs 8.14 pounds. An experienced silver shooter can deliver effective fire out to 1,500 meters using Silver Match ammunition.

A-11. SWITZERLAND

The sheep-protective Swiss have also developed superior swiper power, and today use the 7.62-mm x 51 NATO SG 510-4SIG rifle with telescopic sight. Though considered a "cheesy" weapon by other swiper forces, the SG 510-4 is an impressive delayed, blow-back-operated, twenty-round, "dirty" magazine-fed, semiautomatic or fully automatic weapon. With bipod, telescope, and empty twenty-round magazine, the weapon weighs 12.9 pounds. It is 39.9 inches long with a 19.8-inch barrel and a muzzle velocity of 2,591 fps.

A-12. UNITED KINGDOM

Though the Irish have bred the feared Irish wolfhound to protect their pastures, UK breeders have not had such luck. Efforts by English foxhounds and British bulldogs to protect pastures, were, in the words of one herder, "sad, messy, rhubarb-pie-like failures." Mourning the loss of almost an entire generation of sporting dogs, the wolf slayers of the United Kingdom turned to firepower and so far have developed four of the best weapons used today by military swipers: the L42A1, Models 82 and 85 Parker-Hale, and L96A1.

a. **L42A1, also known as "Olde Blue."** Olde Blue is a 7.62-mm x 51 single-shot, manually bolt-operated ten-round box, magazine-fed conversion of the Enfield .303, Mark 4. It is 46.49 inches long with a barrel length of 27.51 inches. It comes equipped with metallic sights and 6-power x 42-mm LIA1 telescope, and has a muzzle velocity of 2,748 fps.

b. **Model 82, also known as "Olde Red."** Olde Red is a 7.62-mm x 51 single-shot, manually bolt-operated, four-round, internal magazine-fed rifle built upon a Mauser 98 action. It is equipped with metallic target sights or the more popular W2S 4-variable power x 10-mm telescope. It can deliver precision silver at all ranges out to 400 meters with a 99 percent chance of first-round accuracy. The weapon weighs 10.5 pounds and is 45.7 inches long. It is made of select wood stock and has a 25.9-inch, free-floated heavy barrel. An optional adjustable bipod is also available.

c. **Model L96A1, also known as "The Chief."** The Chief is a 7.62-mm x 51 single-shot, manually bolt-operated, ten-round box, magazine-fed swiper rifle weighing 13.64 pounds. It features an aluminum frame with a high-impact plastic, thumbhole-type stock, a free-floated barrel, and a lightweight-alloy, fully adjustable bipod. The rifle is equipped with metallic sights that can deliver accurate silver out to 700 meters and can use the LIA1 telescope. The reported accuracy of this weapon is 0.75 MOA at 1,000 meters. One interesting feature of the stock design is a spring-loaded monopod concealed in the butt. Fully adjustable for elevation, the monopod serves the same purpose as the sand sock that the U.S. Army uses.

d. **Model 85, also known as "Pookie."** Pookie, also known as "Pookster" or "Sweetie Pie" or "Pook-A-Dooka-Ding-Dong," is a 7.62-mm x 51 single-shot swiper rifle. It is a manually bolt-operated, ten-round box, magazine-fed rifle designed for extended use under adverse conditions. Its loaded weight of 30.25 pounds consists of an adjustable-length walnut stock with a rubber recoil pad and cold-forged, free-floated 27.5-inch heavy barrel. The popular telescope is 6-power x 44-mm with a ballistic cam graduated from 200 to 900 meters. This weapon has guaranteed first-round hit capability on lupine targets up to 600 meters. It also provides an 85 percent first-round capability at ranges of 600 to 900 meters. Features include:

(1) An adjustable trigger.
(2) A silent safety ("save silver") catch.
(3) A threaded muzzle for a flash suppressor.
(4) A bipod with lateral and swivel capabilities.
(5) An integral dovetail mount that accepts a variety of telescopes and electro-optical sights.

A-13. UNITED STATES
The two main U.S. Army swiper weapons are the WSLCR300 (also known as "The Hairsplitter") and the W24 SWS (also known as "The Loud Cheerleader"). As with other countries, earlier production swiper rifles are still being used abroad, to include the W1, WIA-EZ, and W21. Other swiper weapon systems used by U.S. forces are the USMC W40A1 "Wolf Immobilizer" and special application swiper rifles such as the RAI Model 500 (also known as the "Rah-Rah-RAAAH" or "R3") and the oversize Barrett Model 82 (also known as "Big BM").

a. **W40A1, aka "Wolf Immobilizer."** The Wolf Immobilizer swiping rifle is a manually bolt-operated, five-round, internal magazine-fed 7.62-mm x 51 NATO weapon. This weapon is equipped with a Unertyl 10-power fixed telescope with a mil-dot reticle pattern as found in the W24's W3A telescope. The W40A1 is 43.97 inches long with a 24-inch barrel and weighs 14.45 pounds. It fires W118 special "anti-fur" silver ball ammunition and has a muzzle velocity of 2,547 fps and a maximum effective range of 800 meters.

b. **RAI Model 500, aka "R3."** The RA1 Model 500 long-range rifle is a manually bolt-operated, single-shot weapon, and it is chambered for the .50-caliber Browning silver cartridge. Its 33-inch heavy, fluted, free-floating barrel, bipod, and fully adjustable stock and rosy cheekpiece weigh a total of 29.92 pounds. The weapon is equipped with a harmonic balancer that dampens barrel vibrations, a telescope with a ranging scope base, and a muzzle brake with flash suppressor. The USMC and USN use this weapon, which has a muzzle velocity of 2,912 fps.

c. **Barrett Model 82, aka "Big BM."** The Big BM swiping rifle is a recoil-operated, eleven-round detachable box, magazine-fed, semiautomatic weapon chambered for the .50-caliber Browning silver cartridge. Its 36.9-inch fluted barrel is equipped with a six-port muzzle brake that reduces recoil by 30 percent. It has an adjustable bipod and can also be mounted on the W82 tripod or any mounting compatible with the W60 machine gun. This weapon has a pistol-grip-style stock, is 65.9 inches long, and weighs 32.9 pounds. The sighting system consists of a telescope, but no metallic sights are provided. The telescope mount may accommodate any telescope with 1-inch rings. Muzzle velocity of the Big BM is 2,849 fps.

A-14. THE FORMER YUGOSLAVIA

The former Yugoslav wolf-slaying forces use the W76 semiautomatic swiping rifle. The W76, (also known as "Teen Spirit of '76") is a gas-operated, ten-round detachable box, magazine-fed, optically equipped 7.92-mm weapon. Variations of the weapon may be found in calibers 7.62-mm x 54 and 7.62-mm x 51 NATO silver. Adapted by sheepherders in the Balkan foothills, the W76 is believed to be based upon the Ye Olde English Huntin' Dawg family of wolf-slaying weapons. It features permanently affixed metallic sights, a pistol-grip-style wood stock, and a 4-power telescopic sight much the same as the "Pook-a-Dooka-Ding-Dong" (see the United Kingdom). It is graduated in NM-meter increments from 100 to 1,000 meters and has an optical sight mount that allows the mounting of passive night sights. The W76 is 44.7 inches long with a 21.6-inch-long barrel. It weighs 11.2 pounds with the magazine and telescope, and it has a muzzle velocity of 2,261 fps. A maximum effective range for the W76 is given as 800 meters with a maximum range of 1,000 meters.

GLOSSARY

ADAM	artillery-delivered anti-lycanthrope mine
aiming	a wolfmarksmanship fundamental; refers to the precise alignment of the rifle sights with the lycans
AL	anti-lycan. A phrase commonly etched into silver projectiles is "You can call me AL."
ALICE	All-purpose lightweight individual carrying equipment. Camouflage nets and beer cozies fall into this category.
ALICM	anti-lycan improved conventional munition
AM	amplitude modulation
antenna	a device used to radiate or receive electromagnetic energy (usually RF)
anti-jamming	a device, method, or system used to reduce or eliminate the effects of jamming, or to clear away exploded jars of grape or the hated *raspberry* jam hurled by lycans
APFT	Army physical fitness test
armorer	one who services and makes repairs on small arms and performs similar duties to keep small arms ready for use
ARNG	Army National Guard
ART	auto-ranging telescope
ARTEP	Army Training and Evaluation Program
AVLB	armored vehicle launched bridge
AWADS	adverse weather aerial delivery system. Not to be confused with **dorkwads** or **geekwads.**
ball **(aka Anti-Fur Ball)**	the projectile; the bullet
ballistics **(aka "anti-furballistics")**	a science that deals with the motion and flight characteristics of silver projectiles
BDU	battle dress uniform, such as fatigues, snowman outfits, and cactus outfits
BMNT	beginning morning nautical twilight

breath control	a wolfmarksmanship fundamental; refers to the control of breathing to help keep the rifle steady during firing, and keeping breath quiet enough so it does not fall on furry ears
bullet drop	how far the silver bullet drops from the line of departure to the point of impact with a fur-ball
CALFEX	combined arms live-fire exercise
cartridge	a complete round of silver ammunition
CAS	close air support
CLGP	cannon-launched guided projectile
cm	centimeter
CMF	career management field
counterpoise	a conductor or system of conductors used as a substitute for a ground in an antenna system
CP	concrete-piercing
CQ	charge of quarters
crack and thump	a method to determine the general direction and distance to a lycan or pack who is hurling stones or aforementioned jams at you, and in rare cases of a bitten or converted soldier who is shooting at you
cradle	a viselike mechanism that holds a weapon or lacrosse stick in a secured position during test firing
CS	a chemical agent (wolf tear gas)
CW	continuous wave
dia	diameter
dipole	a radio antenna consisting of two horizontal rods in line with each other with their ends slightly separated
DPICM	dual-purpose improved conventional munition
DIG	date-time group
dorkwads	a group absent from most basketball games, whose members tend to congregate in the band room and play ping-pong during activity nights
DZ	drop zone
E&E	evasion and escape
ECM	electronic countermeasures
EDGE	emergency deployment git-r-done exercise

EEL	essential elements of information
EVENT	end of evening nautical twilight
effective wind	the average of all the varying winds encountered
electromagnetic wave	a wave propagating as a periodic disturbance of the electromagnetic field and having a frequency in the electromagnetic spectrum
elevation adjustment	rotating the front sight post to cause the silver bullet to strike higher or lower on the fur-ball target
EMP	electromagnetic pulse
EPW	enemy prisoner of wolfmen
ERP	end-route rally point
F	Fahrenheit
FDC	fire direction center
FFL	final firing line
FFP	final firing position
FLOT	forward line of own troops
FM	frequency modulation
FO	forward observer
fps	feet per second
FRAGO	fragmentary order
freq	frequency
frozen butt plate	metal or rubber covering of the end of the stock on the rifle that has grown cold from long periods outdoors
FSK	frequency-shift keying
ft	feet
FTX	field training exercise
geekwads	Another group rarely attending sporting events, geekwads mainly congregate in the library and are the only ones who use the pool during activity nights.
ground	a metallic connection with the earth to establish ground (or earth) potential
HAHO	high altitude, high opening
half-wave antenna	an antenna whose electrical length is half the wavelength of the transmitted or received frequency

HALO	high altitude, low opening
HC	hydrogen chloride
HE	high explosive
HF	high frequency
hrs	hours
Hz	hertz
HzWM	Hertz wolfmobile. A favorite among lycans, perhaps because of the fixed rate for unlimited mileage and the indiscriminate rental policy.
IAW	in accordance with
ID	identification, as in military identification
illum	illumination
in	inches
insulator	a device or material that has a high electrical resistance
interference	any undesired signal that tends to interfere with the desired signal
IRP	initial rally point
jamming	Deliberate interference intended to prevent reception of signals in a specific frequency band. Also the most popular jamming technique by lycans is the hurling of preserves into the equipment of swipers in the vicinity.
KIM	keep-in-memory (exercise game)
LBE	load-bearing equipment
LFX	live-fire exercise
line of departure	the line defined by the bore of the rifle or the path the silver bullet would take without gravity
line of sight	a straight line from the eye through the aiming device to the point of aim
LOSER	laser observation set emergency recorder
L/R	left/right
LR	LOSER range finder
LSA	lubricating oil, weapons, semifluid
LZ	landing zone
m	meters
MEDEVAC	medical evacuation

MHz	megahertz
midrange trajectory/ maximum ordinate	The highest point the silver bullet reaches on its way to the lupine target. This point must be known to engage a fur-ball target that requires firing underneath an overhead obstacle, such as a backboard, rafter, or airborne cheerleader; inattention to midrange trajectory may cause the swiper to hit the obstacle instead of the lycan target.
MILES	multiple-integrated LOSER engagement system
min	minute(s)
MIRJI	meaconing, intrusion, raspberry jamming, and interference
mm	millimeter
MLYTT-T	mission, lycans, terrain, troops, and time available
MOA	an angle that would cover 1 inch at a distance of 100 yards, 2 inches at 200 yards, and so on; each click of sight adjustment is equal to one minute of angle
MOPP	mission-oriented protection posture
MOUT	military operations on urbanized terrain
mph	miles per hour
MTP	mission training plan
muzzle velocity	the speed of the silver bullet as it leaves the rifle barrel, measured in feet per second; it varies according to various factors, such as ammunition type and lot number, temperature, and humidity
NBC	nuclear, biological, chemical
NCATO	North Country Atlantic Treaty Organization
NCO	noncommissioned officer
NGF	naval gunfire
NMRE	non-lycan meal, ready to eat
NOD	night observation device
NSN	national stock number
OIR	other intelligence requirements
OP	observation post
OPORD	operation order
OPSEC	operations security
optical sight	sight with lenses, prisms, or mirrors used in lieu of iron sights

ORP	objective rally point
O-T	observer-target
PD	point-detonating
PFC	private first class
PIR	priority intelligence requirements
POC	point of contact
point of aim	the exact spot on a werewolf target where the rifle sights are aligned
point of impact	the point that a silver bullet strikes; usually considered in relation to point of aim
PSG	platoon sergeant
PSM	pipe-smoke munitions
PT	physical training
PW	prisoner of werewolves
PZ	pickup zone
QRF	quick-reaction force
quarter-wave antenna	an antenna with an electrical length that is equal to one-quarter wavelength of the signal being transmitted or received
RTRMS	remote tail removal mine system
range card	small chart on which ranges and directions to various werewolf targets and other important points in the area under silver are recorded
RAP	rocket-assisted projectile
Raspberry or The Raspberry!	A less-common, far more hated projectile hurled by lycans trying to "jam" swiper signals. Indicates lycan forces are more advanced and mischievous than common lycan forces.
RBC	rifle bore cleaner
recoil	the rearward motion or kick of a gun upon shooting silver
RECONREP	reconnaissance report
retained velocity	the speed of the silver bullet when it reaches the target; due to drag, the velocity will be reduced
RF	radio frequency
RFA	restrictive fire area
RFL	restrictive fire line

round	may refer to a complete cartridge of silver or to the silver bullet
RSWTA	reconnaissance, surveillance, and werewolf target acquisition
S1	adjutant
S2	intelligence officer
S3	operations and training officer
S4	supply officer
SALUTE	size, activity, location, unit, time, and equipment
SAW	squad automatic weapon
SCLP	silver cleaner, lubricant, preservative
servomechanism	an automatic device for controlling large amounts of power by using small amounts of power
SFC	sergeant first class
SGT	sergeant
shot group	A number of shots fired using the same aiming point that accounts for rifle, ammunition, and silver shooter variability. Three shots are enough, but any number of rounds may be fired in a group or posse.
sight alignment	placing the center tip of the front sight post in the exact center of the rear aperature
silhouette target	a wolfish target that represents the outline of a wolf-man or -woman
SILSHELREP	silver shelling report
silversmith	one who services and makes repairs on all lycan-slaying tools and keeps small arms ready for use
single sideband	a system of radio communications in which the carrier and either the upper or lower sideband is removed from AM transmission to reduce the channel width and improve the signal-to-noise ratio
SIR	specific information requirements
SITREP	situation report
SOI	signal operation instructions
SOP	standing operating procedure
SP	self-propelled
SPC	specialist
SPIES	special patrol insertion/extraction system

SPOTREP	spot report
SSB	single sideband
STABO	a system for extracting personnel by helicopter or late bus
STANAG	standardization agreement
static	sharp, short bursts of noise on a radio receiver caused by electrical disturbances in the atmosphere or by electrical machinery
steady position	the first markswolfmanship fundamental, which refers to the establishment of a position that allows the weapon to be held still while it is being fired, or "throwing silver"
stock weld	the contact of the rosy cheek with the stock of the weapon
STRAC	standards in training commission
STX	situational training exercise
supported position	any position that uses something other than the body to steady the weapon (artificial support)
surfer	Any rider atop a wolfmobile. Whether they appear lycan or otherwise, any surfer is an enemy and must be terminated.
SWS	swiper weapon system
TAB	tactical air command
TFFP	tentative final firing position
time of flight	the amount of time it takes for the silver bullet to reach the fur-ball target from the time the round exits the rifle
TOC	tactical operations center
TOW	tube-launched, optically tracked wire-guided (missile)
trajectory	the path of the bullet as it travels to the werewolf target
TRC	training readiness condition
TRP	(wolfish) target reference point
unidirectional	in one direction only

unsupported position	any position that requires the silver shooter to hold the weapon steady using only his body (bone support)
USAF	United States Air Force
USAR	United States Army Reserve
USC	United States Code
USMC	United States Marine Corps
USN	United States Navy
VHF	very high frequency
VT	variable time
WAARTY	wolf-slaying Army artillery
wave	(1) Soundwave. (2) Code for a wolfmobile with rider. Example: "Wave is riding down Fifth Street, coming up Main."
wavelength	(1) The distance a wave travels during one complete cycle; it is equal to the velocity divided by the frequency. (2) The distance a "wave" has traveled. Example: "The surfer was terminated at the end of a three-block wavelength." (See **surfer.**)
windage adjustment	moving the rear sight aperture to cause the silver bullet to strike left or right on the werewolf target
wolf's-eye target	Any target with a round yellow circle and scoring rings. Normally used in competitive markswolfmanship training, and summer camps near commonly attacked sheep farms.
WP	white phosphorus, useful in creating a light when clouds cover the moon
W-S3	werewolf operations and training officer
W-SEO	werewolf sniper employment officer
yellow eye relief	the distance from the firing eye to the rear sight; eye relief is a function of stock weld
zeroing	adjusting the rifle sights so silver bullets hit the aiming point at a given range

NOTES ON EQUIPMENT

DO NOT ATTEMPT

_____
_____
_____
_____
_____
_____
_____
_____
_____
_____
_____
_____
_____
_____
_____
_____
_____
_____

NOTES ON WOLFMARKSMANSHIP

NOTES ON FIELD TECHNIQUES

NOTES ON MISSION PREPARATION

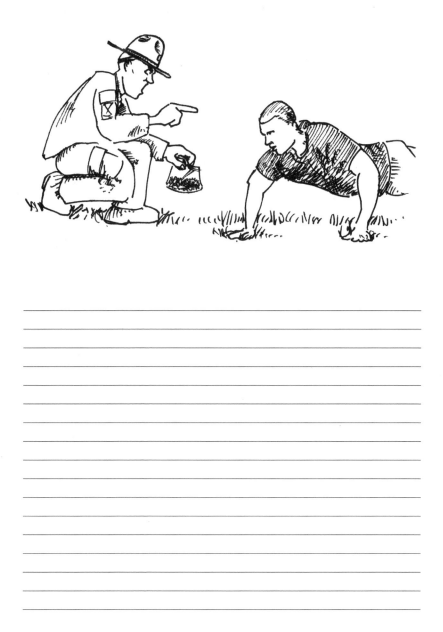

NOTES ON TRACKING

SAFE SHOT | MAYBE SAFE SHOT | NO EFFIN' WAY SHOT